THE OCCULT REVOLUTION

THE OCCULT REVOLUTION

A Christian Meditation

Richard Woods, O.P.

A CROSSROAD BOOK
THE SEABURY PRESS · NEW YORK

1973
THE SEABURY PRESS
815 Second Avenue
New York, N.Y. 10017

Grateful acknowledgement is made to Rod McKuen for permission to reprint the excerpt from "Something Beyond," in *The World of Rod McKuen,* published by Random House, Inc., © 1968; and to United Artists for permission to reprint excerpts from *Hair,* by Gerome Ragni and James Rado, © 1969.

Library of Congress Catalog Card Number: 71-167866
© 1971 by Herder and Herder, Inc.
Manufactured in the United States
ISBN: 0-8164-2584-1

Contents

Introduction   9

1. The Occult Revolution   15
2. The Magic World of Occultism   29
3. Sorcerie, Magitians, and Negromantick Bookes   43
4. Astrology—The Once and Future Thing   58
5. The Celestial Machinery and How It Works   77
6. Witchcraft—The Old Religion as a New Cult   96
7. A Rumor of Devils   121
8. Divination and the Future   146
9. The Dawn of Mind   160
10. Behind the Occult Revolution—A Place Called
    Anomie   179
11. Christ and the Powers   192
12. Mystics and Mod Jesters   216

Afterword   234
Index   238

To

MY AUNT, MARION SHEPHERD,
WHO, IF THERE IS NO SUCH THING AS LUCK,
IS MOST REMARKABLY IN TUNE WITH THE
WORLD,

AND

BISHOP JAMES A. PIKE, LATE OF THE EARTH-PLANE, WHOSE
JOURNEY TOWARDS TRUTH LED HIM ALONG UN-
ACCUSTOMED PATHS, A MODERN WISE MAN
WORTHY OF MEMBERSHIP IN THE BROTHER-
HOOD OF THE MAGI.

Introduction

For the first time in human history, mankind has at hand the means to obliterate civilization totally and possibly destroy all life on earth. The age-old dream of achieving ultimate power, the aim of both magic and technology, has realized a nightmare. If apocalyptic novels, films, and the jeremiads of scientists, religious leaders, and humanitarians have made little impression on popular imagination of the full import of this fact, it is probably because it is all but inconceivable. Devastation by nuclear war is nevertheless a very real possibility and by that fact alone a major transformation of history has taken place within this generation.

A less abrupt form of catastrophy, but equally as lethal, is a population expansion without limit. Moreover, runaway technological "progress" may soon exhaust the earth's natural resources, and the depleted land will waste to death long before its allotted time. Some ecologists (the "catastrophists") allow the race as little as twenty-five years in which to surmount the environmental crisis or be extinguished with all other living species.

Whether with a bang or a whimper, then, the world may end at man's own hand before the turn of this century. Are there alternatives?

The enormity of the tasks confronting the world may require that the political and cultural systems of every nation be altered. Indeed, we may be unable to escape authoritarianism or to avoid the "ecological totalitarianism" feared by Aldous Huxley in *Brave New World Revisited* which is now returning to haunt us. But whatever the cost, we cannot cope with titanic global problems if we are equipped only with the conceptual prejudices and emotional fetishes of centuries or even generations ago. Ultimately, the price exacted of us will depend on how soon we sincerely come to grips with the crises besetting mankind.

We are destined in the best of times to experience in full force the personal and social repercussions of sudden and tremendous change. As a result, insecurity, conservatism will grow in strength, especially in matters of religious belief and practice, as the cosmos trembles under the impact of "future shock."

Obviously, such a state of things is not a portrait of a possible future—it is a candid picture of the present. There is hardly a sector of contemporary life not in the throes of disruption: dropouts, drugs, and dynamite in the schools (and little education); in political life, extremism and apathy alongside of war and civil rebellion; an economy straddled by both affluence and depression; organized religion in a sharp decline during the very time of a flowering of pentecostalism and heterodox cults.

This last aspect of contemporary life, amply documented by all the media, provides an unmistakable index to the profundity and breadth of current social disintegration. History, anthropology, sociology, and psychology testify that religion is the bedrock of social security in all civilizations, or, to recall Peter Berger's phrase, it is the "sacred canopy" which shelters society from the shock waves of change. The more drastic this change, the more fundamental must be the religious response. It is not an accident of history that pentecostalism blossomed again, especially within the Catholic Church, in the aftermath of the Second Vatican Council. (Significantly, the last similar burst of pentecostal fervor followed the Protestant Reformation.) Nor is it by chance that the occult sciences and black arts have also recently reappeared. For properly understood, these forms of belief and behavior are fundamentally *religious*, differing mainly from other orthodox cults to the degree that their devotees accept traditional religious beliefs and practices.

This, briefly, is the underlying presupposition of the present work, one that will, needless to say, require fuller investigation. The "occult revolution" represents a religious response to the impact of technological change in the face of the failure of the churches to provide acceptable values for belief and commitment. The occult is not merely an affront to science and an attack on organized religion; it is the product of their default and a substitute for both.

Thus the current occult revival is symptomatic of a massive "trust gap" that has reached desperate proportions. A growing number of people in the world are rejecting customary values and, unable to formulate another system, are turning to the childhood fantasies of the race in a quest for security—not specifically psychological or sociological security, but religious certainty that there is meaning and order in the universe and in history even if it is humanly possible to glimpse only a fraction of it. Belief in the prevalance of order (the Greek *kosmos*) over chaos (another Greek word) is the social contribution of ritual, myth and magic and, above all, of religion throughout the ages of mankind.

On the debit side, belief in superhuman agencies that control and direct the course of cosmic and world events absolves the believer from responsibility for history while providing an explanation of it. Knowing the secret truths of matter and spirit also admits the possibility of using that knowledge for gain or power—the ambition of the magician and often of the priest. True magic begins with the next step: using the powers that govern the universe to project the power derived from knowledge to actual domination, to become "like gods."

The occult revolution is a signal of change, both past and coming. For if the fabric of life in civil and ecclesiastical society is unravelling, a new pattern is appearing elsewhere and occultism is part of the pattern, however provisional. Its apparently macabre mien belies an important consideration: it, like literature, music,

11

film, economics, youth culture, religious sectarianism, and the very sober reflections of scientists and philosophers, heralds the invasion of the present by the future. The impact is producing some palpable shocks which have been documented by Alvin Toffler and verified, celebrated, explored, and deplored by others.

This meditation is an attempt to account for the future shock-produced occult revolution in a Christian perspective, not as it is important in itself for sociological or psychological or even historical reasons, but as a theologically significant event regarding the shape and meaning of Christian life today and in the future. Above all, it should be continually borne in mind that a "meditation" is not a treatise or a thesis, but rather a form of play. No matter how grim the scrimmage, life for a Christian is still a comedy—even if the divine element in man lends him the trappings of tragic demeanor. Therefore, the following is an offering to be enjoyed, despite the occasional unintentional lapses into high seriousness.

I wish to thank Sister Laurian Pieterek, FSPA, for her support, encouragement, and assistance in preparing this meditation. No doubt, there are many more friends whom I should mention whose patience, aid and interest have enabled me to persevere, but most especially Juliette Peavy, Jerome O'Leary, O.P., and Miss Shirley Hines. I am also indebted to the Chicago chapter of the Process Church of the Final Judgment, who graciously provided information and examined parts of this manuscript in order to assure its accuracy. Material relevant to the Process Church is offered with its consent and approval. Whatever inaccuracies and misrepresentation occur in these pages are the sole responsibility of the author.

THE OCCULT REVOLUTION

1.

The Occult Revolution

Hair: The Revolution Is On

HAIR burst on America like a psychedelic Fourth of July—a playfully perverse celebration of an often factually perverse social situation. Tame as *Hair* may be by now, cultural historians may well reckon it a turning point, not only of American theater, but of American life. For *Hair* proleptically captured the tragicomic exuberance of the flower-children of the late sixties as well as the impotent malaise of their parents—all caught in the grip of civil and family discord, a futile, bloody war, a depressing economy, and the relentless encroachment of technocratic domination.

Political and social criticism and the fragile optimism of an uprooted generation were not the only significant precipitate (however contagious) in the extensive fall-out from *Hair*. Its advent in 1967 also revealed to the "straight" world what had been forgotten for centuries save by that ancient order of stargazers and arcane mathematicians known derisively to the modern age as astrologers: a great world-age is ending and another is about to dawn. This generation is destined to witness the first glimmerings of the Age of Aquarius. It is also doomed to wander in the gloaming of the Age of Pisces—mythically, the era of Christianity.

Other astrological themes and echoes of general occultism pervaded everything from *Hair*'s set design to the broadsheets

15

flung to worldwide audiences. Adepts relished what escaped most of us: astrology, Tarot cards, witchcraft, palmistry, numerology, even devil-worship were *already* a subcultural motif. And, as the eager world of fashion and fun had embraced the beads, flowers, incense, and pot of the hippies, soon zodiac jewelry, computerized horoscopes, and public exorcisms became commonplace.

Of course *Hair* was not primarily concerned with the occult; the war, political incredibility, the generation gap, racism, the drug culture, even the ecological crisis were far more noteworthy themes. Nevertheless, despite the confusion of currents in the watershed, *Hair* certainly marks the reappearance of occultism on the public scene, a movement which had been in high gear with the publication of *Rosemary's Baby* and was well under way with the refilming of horror film classics in the fifties, along with pre-seal-of-approval comics and the syndicated prognostications of Jeane Dixon. But the reappearance of the occult in the seventies is a worldwide phenomenon, not just a NATO atavism; Edgar Mitchell's telepathic experiments with Chicago seer Olaf Jonsson during the flight of Apollo 14 has perhaps made the occult revolution a cosmic affair.

At this early point we are apt to inquire that since the Asian and Middle Eastern wars, the on-going battle for civil rights, poverty and hunger, environmental destruction, inflation, birth control, bombings and threats, kidnappings, women's liberation, increasing crime rates, student uprisings and armed repression, and so many other serious problems clamor for attention and immediate action, why should anyone occupy themselves with the revival of occultism? Especially, perhaps, a Christian?

The answer is not simple. Briefly stated, occultism should be taken seriously, for behind its apparent foolishness and surface dangers lies a severe indictment of contemporary society, especially organized religion, science and politics. For many Christians, the occult revolution seriously challenges the life of faith,

16

presenting a novel problem for urban pastors, teachers, worried parents and even the police. Of course, mere numbers of people involved can never constitute the chief criterion of a social problem for the Church, because every human concern or event is a matter of importance for the Gospel of Christ, the lesser situations of day-to-day existence as well as weighty issues and great crises of nations and peoples. Nevertheless, an involvement of considerable numbers of people complicates most issues, and the occult is no exception.

There is further cause for a meditative reflection on the significance of the occult revolution. As a concrete indictment of contemporary religion, occultism has the power of a counter-cultural agency, particularly for the young—teenage high school students and college youths—who, in their search for meaningful religious *experience* and personal communion, have turned, not only from the churches and synagogues, but also from the promises of science and the vapid allurements of political power, to seek them in drugs, Woodstock Nation, and now in the gnostic climes of esoteric cults.

Certainly the alienated youth who have dropped out of the drug scene ("Speed kills") and radical political activism (notably after the homicidal bombing of the University of Wisconsin's Sterling Hall) or who are turned off by the savagery of the cybernetic jungle, do not constitute a majority or even a sizable minority of American or world youth. There are still thousands of students eager to fill the proliferating vacancies within the technocracy, thousands more who are entering the political arena in orthodox and radical-militant fashion, and hundreds of thousands who are and will ever remain "straight." But ever increasingly have the hippies, the militant radicals, the drug freaks and losers, the alienated and frustrated, and very many ordinary young people conglomerated into witch covens, satanist churches, spiritualist schools, yoga temples, fundamentalist mini-sects (the "Jesus freaks"), and, on the outer limit, the burgeoning

17

movement called pentecostalism. From Hell's Angels to the Children of God, such groups may seem to have little in common, save their emergence at this juncture of time and space, with its definite sociological, psychological and religious significance not only for America but for the world and certainly for the Church. Nevertheless, it may also be that the simultaneity of their appearance has a specific meaning and that their similarities function on a less than obvious dimension.

Religious interest in modern occultism can warrant theological investigation, replete with sociological insights and psychological theories. It may also take the form of pastoral concern. While distinct, the pastoral dimension should in this case (as in all others) be rooted in a theological and socioscientific appraisal of the situation, lest more harm than good result from well-meant but futile accusations, harangues and rescue missions. There is doubtless an element of moral and even physical danger in occultism, but it is worse than useless to assault the matter frontally, for what harm there is operates behind a phalanx of socio-psychological fringe-benefits that are of tangible worth to those involved.

The chief danger in the occult revolution consists in the capitulation of free decision-making and responsibility that inevitably follows the espousal of esoteric cultism with its more or less implicit claims on loyalty and credence. This includes the matron with her horoscopes as well as the apprentice witch in her early teens. Thus a secondary theme of this meditation will be the risk implied in the attempt to rediscover meaning and place in the manifestly chaotic jumble of contemporary history: the occultist, by accepting the belief that superhuman agencies direct the fate of man and nature and must be obeyed or brought into subjection, abdicates his own obligation for creating history. In the bargain he loses at least the exercise of personal self-determination and exposes himself to the control of powers outside himself, whether conceived of as personal demons or social

18

forces. Attempting to escape from a meaningless existence leads not only in a circle, but deeper into futility. There is no escape from life.

Counterfeit faith is perhaps worse than no faith because false coinage may even fool the counterfeiter. Idolatry was forbidden in the Judaeo-Christian tradition not only because such worship distracted the faithful from the cult of the Lord God, but also because the gods to whom they turned were, in fact, "unknown gods" as well as strange gods. It was not without precedent, then, that for Paul, Augustine, Thomas Aquinas, and the major theological tradition of the Christian Church, occult beliefs and practices ranked among the sins of idolatry as well as false worship, both faithless and sacrilegious.

Today we are more inclined to define idolatry less dramatically, as the attempt, for instance, to find ultimate meaning in the provisional or illusory. Our problem is to determine the idolatrous from the merely mistaken, the injurious from the silly, as well as the true from the false. For undoubtedly much commonly considered occult belief or superstitious practice may be neither irreligious nor pathological; it may be humane and beneficial. Oriental religions and philosophical disciplines, especially yoga, Zen Buddhism, and Taoism; astral influences, ESP and prophecy, unidentified flying objects and perhaps many other beliefs and phenomena are the spiritual patrimony of millions of wise, reasonable and loving human persons, or matters scientists are now seriously attempting to fathom.

What, then, is the occult revolution? How does occultism differ from ordinary experience? And how, above all, for the present inquiry, is the occult related to religious experience and the rise of the counter culture? The attempt to deal with these questions will occupy the remainder of this meditation. First, we will look at modern occultism in its revolutionary, counter-cultural exuberance, then settle in for a more leisurely excursion into the main areas of occultism from astrology to witchcraft. The second

19

portion of our reflection will turn to the significance of the occult revolution, its impact on society and religion, its causes and consequences. Finally, we will endeavor to reckon with the pastoral problems engendered in the heat of revolt.

Our patrons through this journey should, in all fairness, be the elusive Magi of St. Matthew's Gospel, who, despite the royal robes later tradition foisted on them to cover up their magicians' apparel in more respectable fashion, were quite simply a group of astrologers. Yet for reasons known only to God and St. Matthew, they were chosen to represent the gentile nations in paying first homage to the Christ.

The Passion for the Occult

Although writing of love, Denis de Rougemont no doubt had our present concern in mind when he wrote, "The greatest pill in the world today is the passion for the occult." Doctors are indeed becoming alarmed at the numbers of seriously sick persons, including the blind and cancer-ridden, who consult "healers" who possess, or claim to possess, psychic rather than medical powers. In the November 1970 issue of *Today's Health,* published by the American Medical Association, we are told: "Those desperate, and others with blind faith, often do feel better temporarily after visiting mumbo-jumbo practitioners. But this, of course, could deter them from seeking urgently needed legitimate help." Many have died as a consequence of believing in such charlatanry, others have been made worse than they were. But some have been cured: the problem is not simply one of quackery. At any rate, fakes as well as sincere and sometimes successful healers are cropping up in every major American city and the hopeful are flocking to them—a portent of the occult revolution.

Everywhere we are struck by similar symptoms of the reappearance of arcane arts and psychic sciences, widespread in-

pathic communication and clairvoyance, telekinesis and levitation, which are no longer considered "occult," although most people continue to think of them as such. Whether that makes them more or less understandable to the average citizen than Einstein's physics, the Salk vaccine, or cybernetics is open to question. Among the brahmins tending the sacred cattle of "science," however, there is good evidence of a change in attitude from the ridicule and enmity with which Joseph B. Rhine was met by his professional colleagues to one of reserved suspicion or even receptivity.

Among amateurs, a new yen for the occult is no less pronounced; in this instance the revolution is a popular uprising. In the starry realms, writers have estimated that as many as 175,000 Americans dabble in astrology. At least two out of three daily newspapers run astrological columns, both man-devised and computer-programmed which means somewhere in the neighborhood of 1800. Adding the semi-weeklies and monthlies, that number would exceed by far the modest 2000 suggested by Pauwels and Bergier. By comparison, in any event, just a few decades ago less than ninety of America's 1750 papers had similar columns. Almanacs, however, ran astrological articles and still do, despite their professed skepticism regarding the validity of predictions. To this printed matter, add the raw tonnage of jewelry, posters, games, decorations, paperweights, and the rest of the commercial excreta evoked by the current fashionableness of occultism, and we have indeed the material evidence of a social revolution in values and attitudes.

Historically, of course, there is also evidence that occultism has always hovered on the outskirts of social respectability, and we might thereby be tempted to conclude that today's novelty is simply the burgeoning popularity of a fad. Such an easy deduction hides a problem: distinguishing between what is and what is not occult would then become merely a matter of determining how much of the population shares a given belief or behaves in specific ways, whereas nominally, at least, "occult" denotes "hidden"—presumably from the masses. Logically, at least, mere popularity or acceptability seems insufficient to define the occult, less sufficient than, for instance, they would be in matters of fashion or politics. Moreover, such criteria cannot explain the causes of the occult revolution, however much it can be sampled statistically. Hence we still are left pondering: what is the occult?

Negatively, occultism does not seem to be merely an extension of the perpetual obsession of the few with birth charts or fortune-tellers, or, on the other hand, the wider-ranging psychological fallout from horror movies, comic books, TV monster comedies, and witchcraft serials. More likely, *Rosemary's Baby, Dark Shadows,* and *The Hulk* themselves result from the public's new attitude towards the occult, given the business instincts of Hollywood and the video barons.

But even granting general fascination with the dark side of the human psyche, which delights and shudders when faced with the unknown, cherishes such gothic classics as *Frankenstein* and *Dracula,* and revels vicariously with the mini-ghouls haunting suburban lanes on Halloween, there must be something positive, some affirming value to warrant the upswing in popular occultism. My own estimation is that it is to be found in a newly experienced thirst for transcendence, immortality and liberation —a desire which has its source in other, antecedent conditions, scientific innovations, profound changes in society, the religious upheavals of the sixties, all of which will eventually make their influence felt in manifold ways. The quest for the supernatural implied in occult dabbling indicates that this new force is, as many have intuited, a religion, or, more accurately, a counter religion. Therefore, as a religious factor of a counter-cultural bent, the occult revolution is also a cultural event, for religions are essential factors in every culture. At this point, let us take a closer look at the cult of transcendence and the rag-bag contents of occultism.

Drugs, Daemons, and the Desire for Transcendence

In *Hair,* the chorus in a moment of solemn euphoria salutes marijuana and the hallucinogenic sacraments of the counter culture:

> *My body*
> *Is walking in space.*
> *My soul's in orbit*
> *With God, face to face.*[2]

Similarly, but in more homely metaphor, Rod McKuen's lyric "Something Beyond" expresses the same longing for transcendent experience:

> *Beyond the day, beyond the day,*
> *Beyond the 33rd of April*
> *And the 41st of May,*
> *It well may be I'll never come*
> *To see the secret secrets*
> *Of the darker part of me,*
> *But I'll keep looking till*
> *The need to look is gone.*
> *My arms reach out toward*
> *Something Beyond.*[3]

It may be argued that since man first looked into the spangled miracle of the night sky, he has longed for "something beyond" his normal day-to-day experiences. But compared to the spiritual pabulum of popular music the ilk of "I Believe," the preceding lyrics are remarkably lofty—the first being an unorthodox, unabashed celebration of chemical ecstasy, the second a simple,

---

[2] Gerome Ragni and James Rado, *Hair,* New York, 1969, page 144.
[3] *The World of Rod McKuen,* New York, 1968, page 99.

agnostic paean extolling fidelity to the inner search. Today's youth are not noted for harkening to easy answers from the past, except experimental modes such as trance-worship, to make contact with something beyond ordinary human capabilities. Without sure guides, the quest itself becomes all important, and the goal may become quite incomprehensible.

An American astrologer, Dane Rudhyar, explains: "All humanity is caught in a condition of collective crisis. It is because of this that men are seeking more than ever to comprehend any type of 'threshold knowledge,' occultism, astrology—anything which might lead to a new sense of living, a new understanding."[4] The "collective crisis" motif will reappear later; here it is sufficient to note that occultism, with its ancient history of unorthodox creeds and cult, and above all its consistent assertion of the existence of powers emanating from "beyond," is more in tune with the contemporary quest for transcendence than more traditional beliefs and practices.

While McKuen cannot be considered an occultist, *Hair,* as we have seen, determinedly blends psychedelia, drugs, and the occult with stage decor and exotic metaphysical allusions. Two cards from the ancient Tarot deck figure prominently in the musical. "The Magician," which is reproduced as a huge banner dominating the set as the lights come up, symbolizes immortal life, man's will in communion with divine power, manifesting the inner nature of reality through human self-consciousness. Later during the program, the cast distributes a broadside to the audience. It is another Tarot card, "The Lovers," representing human love under divine benediction. Beauty, harmony, and happiness radiate from the naked, primeval lovers and from the god-like angel above them.

These cards and their mystical interpretation adequately summarize *Hair's* central psychological themes, its positive statements about life, possibly explaining the show's amazing popu-

[4] *The Practice of Astrology,* Baltimore, 1970, page 23.

larity among the young throughout the world. For it is now unquestionably evident that the great numbers of students who turned to the sexual freedom, drugs, and communal living explored in *Hair* are members of an international movement, a collective search for meaning and security in a world bequeathed to them rife with chaos and uncertainty, desensitized and ravaged by industrial exploitation no less than political brinksmanship. Margaret Mead portrays their anguished state of mind: "Can I commit my life to anything? Is there anything in human cultures as they exist today worth saving, worth committing myself to?" She goes on to summarize precisely the gravity of the contemporary crisis: "Just as man is newly faced with the responsibility for not destroying the human race and all living things and for using his accumulated knowledge to build a safe world, so at this moment the individual is freed to stand aside and question, not only his belief in God, his belief in science, or his belief in socialism, but his belief in anything at all."[5]

A heady temptation for the young: to reject the parental culture's values in view of the mess handed them in the form of war, famine, poverty, ecological trauma, injustice, the moronic struggle for material comfort and power. Their broadcast questioning already implies a negation of very serious proportions.

But total skepticism is a difficult feat to ask of the young, even as their world seems to crumble about them. The will to believe is strong, perhaps as strong as the desire to reject customary values which are obviously bankrupt. Hence arises the possibility and perhaps need to believe in "something *beyond*" the pale of those values, and this provides a connection between the rise of occultism and the appearance of other movements, thus mitigating rejection with hope. That the British psychiatrist R. D. Laing, an increasingly local spokesman for the counter culture in England, has been appealed to by historians of the

[5] *Culture and Commitment*, New York, 1970, page 10.

occult as well regarding the normalcy of "other" states of mind than those usually considered "sane," can be taken as a clue to the sociological significance of modern occultism. It is a counter-cultural phenomenon; in my opinion, a folk religion resuscitated to countermand the claims of organized churches. But here we are running ahead of our inquiry. We have yet to rifle the mixed bag of occultism and attempt to sort out the weird panoply of beliefs, claims, practices, and cults that have drawn many of the world's young rebels into their sphere.

Such an undertaking will involve us, first of all, in magic, for the occult revolution begins in a world of mysterious events, unseen forces and laws that transcend our normal understanding of workaday life. Following this mystical tour, we will encounter the major forms of occultism: astrology, witchcraft and sorcery, devil-worship, divination, and around the twilit edges, a glimpse of unidentifiable flying objects, paranormal experiences, prophecy, and perhaps an occasional monster.

2.

The Magic World of Occultism

In the November 1970 issue of the American Medical Association's magazine *Today's Health* already referred to, mention is made of the widely accepted opinion that "Occult practices and philosophies embrace everything from Hindu karma to reincarnation, numerology, pseudo-religions, and seers with 'psychic vibrations.'" Such a fluid category can and often does include everything from alchemy to Zen under one wet blanket of opprobrium whether or not the arts, sciences, practices, beliefs, and formulae have anything in common. Yoga and Zen Buddhism are not occult, no matter how esoteric—they are religious and philosophical doctrines and ways of life which have nothing to do with witchcraft, magic, predicting the future, and other commonly associated tricks (though the cultures in which these teachings originated may have their own magical traditions, and so on). Like hypnosis, extrasensory perception is now the subject of serious scientific research and application and is not an occult art no matter how mysterious it may be. Stage hypnotism cannot invalidate the psychiatric or medicinal employment of hypnosis, nor does aerodynamics become an occult science because a contemporary witch rides to a Sabbath on a jet-liner.

Given the propensity for uncritical pigeon-holing, even in the dovecotes of universities and research clinics, it is not in the least surprising to encounter it when dealing with the occult, at best an elusive, mystery-laden collect defying easy categorization. Deriving from a Latin word meaning "to cover up or hide," occult usually refers to arts and practices involving the use of divination, magical formulae, and the like. Thus spake the dictionary, which is not much help. The key word and most basic common factor in all definitions of the occult is "magic," however, which is no easier to define than the former term. Non-theatrical magic—that is, true magic, which is to entertainment what karate is to televised wrestling—is the art of employing the mysterious, supernatural forces believed to underpin the universe in order to produce desired effects at will. This requires explanation, but for the sake of clarity and convenience, henceforward occult sciences and arts will be considered those which depend on a magical conception of the nature and structure of the universe and everything in it including mankind.

Magic is as old as man, and belief in it is the archaic patrimony of every civilization. Fragments of magical belief and practice appear at every level of life, like the shards of ancient pots mixed with the mortar of Athens and Rome. Ground-breaking ceremonies, ship-launchings, dedicatory and funeral rites such as the placing of stones (tombstones, cornerstones, and the like), stopping the clock at the moment of death; birthday parties and toasts; fear of black cats, the number thirteen, toads, bats and snakes; the naming of months and seasons, days of the week, the construction of the calendar, the very reckoning of time—all were originally magical. Most superstitions—a word which literally means "left-over"—are ritualized patterns of magical behavior, the reasons for which have been obscured by centuries of custom. A person may never know exactly why nailing a horseshoe to the doorframe or carrying a rabbit's foot brings luck, but to those whom such practices are meaningful, reasons are not as important as are results or at least belief—whether in the charm or perhaps just in luck itself. "Chance is the god of the indolent." (Horseshoes, incidentally, are a potent defense against witches, who fear iron. Further, horses were traditionally considered particularly vulnerable to hexes and were therefore protected by charms. By a curious turn of thought, known as apotropaic magic, the horse's shoe became an anti-witch charm. The rabbit's foot was originally a young man's amulet for attracting a girl's love, with its obvious associations with fecundity and amorous adventures.)

Magic and Men's Minds

Beyond the familiar landscapes of all our minds, preoccupied with electric toothbrushes, lunar modules, people, pets and world problems, there lies a shadowy land of witches and dragons, talking animals and malevolent spirits, and the law here is a magical one. Early psychiatrists and psychologists, including Freud and pre-eminently Jung, illuminated some of this realm for us, but we are better acquainted with its hidden mysteries from our own childhood fantasies, fairy tales and the fears of dark places and strange noises. We still take our ids out for a run in these fabulous stretches whether we attend a double-feature horror film or curl up with a gothic mystery or science-fiction novel or even a monster comic book.

This subterranean world of our personality is not all harmless fun and scary children's games. It touches the edges of our deepest religious feelings and aspirations but also extends along the borders of madness to that bone-cold territory where death lurks to terrify our unguarded moments of wonder, when we ponder life and meaning. It reverberates with dread tension as we stare out beyond the stars and galaxies to the mysterious quasars, pulsars, "collapsars," and further into the infinite void from which no light beckons.

Quite simply, all men seem to possess a deep and inescapably powerful dimension of mind or spirit which thrills in the presence of the unknown or uncanny. There is a story told of a government computer somewhere in the Rockies which is installed

31

on a raised dais in a semi-darkened room. Colored lights play over its twinkling panels amid subdued chirpings and beeps. Such an atmosphere of tomb or temple is the environment in which mankind has always enclosed what it finds awesome and powerful. The perceived presence of the "nebulous" elicits reverence or fear, whether the object of adoration is an invisible god or a chunk of rock, a mystical flame or an analog computer.

Man is a utilitarian creature, however, and in worshiping, contemplating and even penetrating the unknown, he has always desired to harness and direct its power, or at least to render such forces that be either benevolent or at least harmless. Gods and computers alike, as well as electricity, psychology, and various other powers and principalities, have been employed to create an easier and more humane world.

Bronislaw Malinowski, the famous anthropologist of the Trobriand Islands, relates in his study *Magic, Science and Religion,* that "Early man seeks above all to control the course of nature for practical ends, and he does it directly, by rite and spell, compelling wind and weather, animals and crops to obey his will. Only much later, finding the limitations of his magical might, does he in fear or hope, in supplication or defiance, appeal to higher beings; that is, to demons, ancestor-spirits, or gods."[1]

Archaic Magic

Our first encounter, then, in the pre-historical mists of man's dawning is not with the sorcerer who relies on the aid of demons, or with the priest who conjures by the gods, but with the half-sinister magician, the man of personal power. There seems to have been no culture devoid of his influence and even today in primitive societies the shaman or medicine-man, the *brujo* or witch doctor, still shares the seat of authority with kings and priests, and against whom the efforts of the Church and

[1] New York, 1954, page 19

32

state are at best only partially effective. And not without cause, for often the magician is the only "wise man" whose power can ward off the terrors that modern civilization and theology deny, such as attacks by demons and witches, and also the ravages of disease and injury, especially in those many areas where no doctor can—or will—venture.

Some years ago I accompanied a Spanish nursing sister to a hut in the Andean wilderness of Bolivia to treat a young Indian whose leg had been fractured a month before. The young man's father, the village *brujo* (who was pointedly absent), had set the compound fracture, cleaned and sutured the wound with ordinary thread, then dressed and splintered the leg and positioned it expertly on supports to permit comfort but not movement. There was no trace of infection despite the mud floor, the sooty walls and the ever present animals in the hut. The bone was mending well. (The nurse spent the rest of the morning, however, giving injections of penicillin, especially to infants born with syphilis—the kind of malady beyond the magician's ken.)

Magic is far older than civilization. On the walls of caves in Lascaux, LaMouthe and Niaux, France, and in Altamira, Spain, there have been discovered remarkable likenesses of bison, boars, horses, and deer dating from the Paleolithic period, some thirty thousand years ago. These paintings are our first evidence not only of human art, but also of magic. From what we can surmise from the paintings themselves, a designated artist, perhaps a prototype of the magician, drew a likeness of an animal soon to be hunted. For the primitive mind, an image is linked to the object represented, and consequently when the artist or perhaps the hunters drew arrows, spears and traps on the animals, or possibly hurled their own weapons and even specially fashioned magical ones at the icons, they believed this would assure their success in the coming hunt.

Contemporaneous aboriginal peoples still engage in similar rituals, an example being the diminutive airstrips and grass airplanes fashioned by the "Cargo Cults" of remote Southern Pacific islands. These, they believe, will bring back the great silver "birds" that once (during World War II) landed on these islands and were disgorged of fabulous treasures. Voodoo cults and even the urban witches of Europe and America abuse images made of wax, clay or cloth and linked to the intended victim by incorporating some of his hair, fingernail clippings or some personal effect. Sometimes merely a reasonable likeness or a verbal charm ("This is Wilbur Abercrombie") establishes the magical connection with the living person. Then, whatever is done to the image should also befall the victim. Unfortunately, the psychological power of this kind of imitative magic is indeed strong enough to prove fatal to those who believe in it.

Rituals, charms, spells, talismans—all the paraphernalia of the magician's craft, are based on several assumptions about life and the nature of the world which seem to be shared by archaic and primitive peoples and most children, as Jean Piaget adequately demonstrated over a lifetime of research.

1. Universal Glue

First, it is a possibly universal belief that underlying all life and the phenomena of nature, whether animals, plants, men or lifeless elements such as storms, mountains and seas, there is an impersonal force, a power called *mana* among the Polynesians and bearing many other names throughout the world. To the philosophers of antiquity, the Aether—that mysterious "fifth essence"—was of similar character. By its all-pervasive presence, *mana* unites everything into one all-embracing whole, although it may be present in varying degree. Magicians, shamans, priests and "prophets," sometimes even madmen and kings, possessed it in an extraordinary degree; the early Greeks and Romans would say that such were possessed of a *daimon* or *genius* (a word related to the Arabian *"djinn"*), a personal spirit under whose tutelage Socrates and the later emperors were believed to teach and rule.

One might be born a shaman or magician, although initiation into a society of medicine-men could also confer power to the primitive neophyte; occasionally, the "gift" of the gods was conferred by a vision or a dream, perhaps by a severe illness or injury, after which the victim was seen to have been "touched." The Romans considered madness to be a sign of divine visitation and called epilepsy "*morbum divinum*"; the archaic Greeks called such states "enthusiasm." We might define them as "obsession." But however it came, certain members of tribe, clan or nation were endowed with special power and had to be reckoned with because whatever is powerful is likewise dangerous. Sometimes epilepsy or madness was occasion for the murder of its unfortunate victim, since demons, too—not the familiar spirits of the sages, but malevolent inferior deities—could touch a person and occupy his body, and thus bring evil upon the people. Belief in demonic possession prevailed well into the nineteenth century in Europe and America and still brings terror to millions of people throughout the world.

2   The Magic Knot

Secondly, by interrelating all the multiple objects, people and events of life, *mana* permits the control or direction of these manifestations of the Oneness that is the All. Thus the quintessential aether was the answer to the riddle of the One and the Many: all the various and apparently distinct things about us, the whole economy of cosmic furniture from mountains to ants, is tied together by invisible strands of power. By discovering *how* the treatment of one cog in this universal mechanism will activate the other parts, primitive man and pre-eminently the magician gave great scope to his power: he caused rain by sprinkling water from a gourd onto a circle of earth; he strength-

35

ened the spirit of the departed by offering food to the corpse; he impeded love-making or diminished bodily vigor by tying knots in a magic cord placed near the victim; he might cure warts by killing toads.

Thus one way in which the "world machine" can be operated is by *imitation*: a cardinal axiom of the archaic and primitive mind is that "like produces like." Two events, persons or things associated even in the mind alone or by means of art have, it is believed, a real connection, thereby giving curses and blessings their force. Anthropologists identify this as imitative or "sympathetic" magic, which is based on correspondences or "sympathies" which permeate the universe. Later magicians were to develop elaborate systems of correspondences, the whole of which resemble a metaphysical telephone exchange. Much of this kind of lore is contained in the Cabala, the body of Jewish occult writings that dates from the third century A.D. to the Middle Ages, when the bulk of the doctrine was codified. Cabalistic material has been extremely influential in the development of magical theories from the nineteenth century onwards by ex-Christian Gentiles such as Eliphas Levi and Aleister Crowley.

Central to cabalistic thought, as well as a distinguished feature of all magic, is the penchant for classifying everything into a master plan—planets, the signs of the Zodiac, numbers, the days of the week, demons, and divinities, metals, colors, flowers, trees and herbs, animals, gems, parts of the body, emotions and passions, diseases, professions and whatever else can fit into a "rational" pattern. Correspondences rule everything. Thus there are twenty-two letters in the Hebrew alphabet, twenty-two cards in the Major Arcana of the Tarot deck, twenty-two books of the Hebrew Bible, and—not by chance—twenty-two chapters of Revelation, Augustine's *City of God,* and the magical grimoires of Levi and Crowley. Among the correspondences that exist among natural things, one (of the major seven) includes the Sun, Sunday, yellow, gold, saffron, sunflowers, the bay tree, parsley and nettles, the lion (and astrological sign Leo), the back and spine, the numeral One and, therefore, God (Adonai), the demon Sorath, the male principle, spirit, mind, royalty, politics, and much, much more. (The study of magic is obviously not for those of an unsystematic disposition!)

The other major kind of magic involves the transmission of power by direct contact and is called *contagious* magic. By eating the heart of a slain enemy, the warrior gains strength; in certain Australian tribes, a younger sibling could be killed and fed to an older ailing infant to impart health and strength; washing in water cleanses from moral impurity by extension; eating the totemic animal establishes sacred communion among the members of the clan; applying certain herbs to injured or diseased parts of the body effects cures; sacrificing human victims to the sun insures its victory over the power of darkness during an eclipse by nourishing it with the blood of life.

Herein lies the basis of all sacramental ritual in all the world's religions, and extant versions of such practices, which easily cross the border back into magical superstition, are derived from sacramental rites: crossing oneself in times of danger, wearing talismans or medals for protection or "luck," burning blessed palms or candles for protection in a storm—thus extending the sacred time of Palm Sunday or Candlemas. The sacred object spreads an aura of power around itself including those to whom it belongs or touches. The search for such knowledge and skill of application and the transmission of both within a select group of initiates becomes the life's work of the archaic magician, and later of the priest. Indirectly, the methodology and intention are also the source of science and technology: all that is necessary in order to work the world-machine is knowing how the parts relate to one another and finding the handles.

The Supernatural World

The third fundamental belief of archaic and primitive peoples (as well as many civilized megalopolites) is that there exists "another" world invisible to ordinary perception but nevertheless powerfully involved in the affairs of this one. Belief in a higher, "supernatural" realm, similar but vastly superior to our own, probably developed from the observance of certain inexplicable phenomena on the one hand and belief in spirits on the other.

Natural but mysterious events such as earthquakes, volcanoes, geysers, comets and eclipses, the marvel of the changing seasons, the solstices, the paths of the sun and moon and "lesser lights," the regular tides and unpredictable winds, storms and droughts —and much more of the fabric of natural existence—seem to be manifestations of some uncanny, powerful force to a mind unsophisticated by technology and astrophysics. Insurance policies still refer to natural disasters as "acts of God." Sometimes the feeling of awe which such manifestations evoked in archaic man was also produced (as is the case for us) by the star-brilliant summer sky, the sunset or dawn, perhaps by enormous caves or special places such as secluded valleys, groves, and mountain peaks. Death itself, the ultimate mystery, presents a great and baffling enigma: what becomes of the life and personality when the body dies?

Part of the answer came in the form of spirits. A child, Piaget tells us, and a primitive or archaic adult all find the world a congenial home for invisible "presences." Not only animals, but springs, rivers, trees and rocks, mountains and the air itself if not equally "alive" are at least the haunt of natural spirits, beings without bodies but with personality, name, and, above all, power. Storms and natural hazards are the work of demons, bad spirits who lurk in deep caves, the bowels of the earth, dark places or in the sea, the North, the desert, the moors or burial places. But such spirits are not ghosts, for they never had a mortal body—although they could be killed or die, despite great longevity. Sometimes they became visible, appearing either quite ordinary or horrible beyond endurance; sometimes they were "halflings"—diminutive people-like creatures familiar to us from tales: fairies, elves, dwarves, gnomes, goblins, hobgoblins, leprechauns, nymphs, dryads, fauns, and imps, or they could be giants, trolls, and the like. A middle ground between non-human, semi-immortal spirits and ghosts was occupied by ghouls, vampires, and were-animals.

There were other spirits to be reckoned with as well: did not the apparition of a dead relative or loved one in a dream indicate that they, too, had a spirit which survived death? If so, could not ancestors or slain enemies return from the land of the dead as revengeful spirits, maliciously persecuting those who killed them or who had failed to give them due departure ceremonial? Consequently, funeral customs, particularly the details of burial, become matters of utmost importance to all peoples everywhere, from the careful placing of heavy rocks over the grave to prevent the ghost's untimely reappearance to the literally monumental heights of Egyptian culture. Both forms of tomb-building are reflected today in the gravestones and mausoleums that occupy the park-like cemeteries of village hamlet and sprawling metropolis.

The gods, too, were important inhabitants of the "other" land of primitive belief. These vastly superior beings were sometimes identified with the sun, moon, planets, and stars, suggesting that the sky was really the abode of spirits, perhaps even the spirits of the dead, if only those of the god-like heroes who fell in battle. The heavens, then, were a likely site for the supernatural realm, housing not only the celestial bodies but the "place" from which came rain, lightning, thunder, comets, the dew, and snow. The eternal movement of the sun and moon against the starscape was a suitably grandiose theater for re-enacting legendary events, and stories were likewise created to explain the goings-on of the divine actors (demons and the common dead being relegated to the basement of the cosmic theater, the "nether" world below the earth).

Untying the Knot

The gods, immortal, supremely powerful, and now including in their number certain mortals whose deeds on earth had been of god-like valor, were capable of very human characteristics, such as love, hatred, favoritism, revenge, jealousy, and caprice, and they were able to listen to the appeals of living men, to be bargained with, appeased, or even tricked. All this was too much for the meager talents of ordinary tribesmen, even if they were magicians. The supernatural world demanded skilled attention, and the job of dealing with spirits, ghosts, gods, and demons (and if business was dull, the lesser spirits as well) was turned over to a special class of men, the priests, whose otherworldly preoccupations left the magicians free to reckon with more mundane affairs.

Unlike the magician's business of curing, blessing, cursing, protecting from witches and so forth, the priests of old were consecrated for the sole purpose of worship and augury—divining the gods' will, the decrees of Fate. Not only their persons but the instruments of their craft, their dwellings, and place of work became what the word signifies: sacred—set aside. The rest of the world was literally *pro-fanum,* outside the temple and somewhat inferior. Of course, priests and magicians were soon quarrelling and poaching on each others' domains, and primitive science emerged from the controversy, as men eager for understanding tired of the techniques of manipulation or propitiation.

Nevertheless, even for archaic science, the cosmos was a conveniently tiered framework on which the workings of the celestial mechanics could be studied. With the gods ever farther above, the departed and demons below, mortal man became the image of the cosmos, linking the whole scheme in himself. He had a spirit which ascended whence it had come, and a body which was of the earth, earthly. He was the microcosm, reflecting the macrocosmic universe. This view became a principle of supreme importance for the later history of magic, and a cardinal feature of science and religion.

However we reconstruct the worldview of archaic man, even on the basis of extant primitive cultures, which is the proper business of cultural anthropology and the history of religion, it is demonstrable that belief in the supernatural, including gods, ghosts, spirits, and magical power, emerged from the pre-historical millenniums of human consciousness as the wellspring of magic, science, and religion. The attempt to manipulate the powers of the other world is the basis of magical techniques, the desire to adore and serve the manifest Power is the spark of religion, and the refusal to do either coupled with the desire to understand the workings of the universe is the origin of science. But for archaic man, as for primitive men today, these three responses to life are not as sharply divided as we would like to believe they are for us: often the roles of priest, magician or sage merged or collided and would through all coming ages. Occultism is no more than the persistent belief that neither the lofty speculations of theologians nor the discoveries of scientists completely account for the actual events of life, which it is the long-obscured role of the magician to expound. Today's occult revolution is a darkling hint that perhaps science and theology, technology and liturgy, have claimed too much for their attempt completely to suppress the magical element, and life is much more complicated that we have been led to believe in orthodox fashion.

Magic is once again waxing, and out of the haze of the ancient groves and caverns of the Paleolithic era, the half-comic, half-frightening figure of the Sorcerer has emerged to wander the avenues of Chicago and Cape Kennedy. His calling-card may

sympathetic? } 2 types magic
Contagious }

3 times blessed

well be inscribed with the opening lines of the *Emerald Table* of Hermes Trismegistos, the legendary grandson of Adam and founder of all magic and wisdom, himself a god who directed the building of the pyramids: "that above is like that below, and that below is like that above, to achieve the wonders of the One thing."

Hermetica

3.

Sorcerie, Magitians, and Negromatick Bookes

THE romance of sorcery is an ancient human foible, and even the word "magic" is so ancient that it defies translation, as do all our most fundamental concepts. Professor Lynn Thorndike, whose monumental *History of Magic and Experimental Science* has so far taken eight volumes and over five thousand pages to recount, claims that the word originated in the Sumerian or Akkadian "*imga*," meaning "deep" or "profound."[1] Paul Christian, the celebrated French scholar of the nineteenth century, suggested that it derives from the Chaldean "*Maghdim*," meaning "wisdom," or "philosophy."[2] Whatever the linguistic ancestry, the first known practitioners of the magical arts were Chaldean, those ancient "wise men" (which can be rendered "wizards") called *Magi* by the Romans. By the time the Gospel of St. Matthew was composed, a *Magus* was primarily an astrologer or star-diviner, but according to legends, some of them Christian, the Magi were actually a society whose members were simultaneously theologians, sages, and scientists, extending in an unbroken line back to Hermes Trismegistos, identified as the son of Seth, the Egyptian god Thoth and the Romans' Mercury.

The claims of the Magi to universal knowledge with the consequent threat it presented to kings and priests earned them enmity, persecution, and even massacre. Once the ruling caste of

---

[1] New York, 1923; volume I, page 4.
[2] *The History and Practice of Magic,* edited and revised by Ross Nichols, New York, 1969, page 18.

ancient Persia, the Magi eventually became a secret society devoted to discovering the knowledge of the ages and preserving it intact, safe from princes, generals, and pontiffs. What became of the Magi is a fascinating query to the answering of which there has been no dearth of suggestions, but it would take us too far afield to attempt further additions here.

Paul Christian maintains that India was the birthplace of Magism. According to a tradition adopted by many Fathers of the early Church, twelve Magi, descendants of Hermes-Thoth, thrice-blest son of Seth, the son of Adam, awaited on the pinnacle of Mount Victory for the coming of the promised Messiah. For a year at a time, three of the Twelve would scan the sky for a sign in the stars that the Christ had been born. Though extremely long-lived, when death claimed one of their number the Magi replenished the Twelve from the ranks of their closest followers. High (and dry) in the mountains, they survived even the Deluge.

Wherever it began, the cult of Magism eventually spread to the Middle East before the time of Christ. In Persia, the Magi attempted to wrest control of the monarchy after the death of Cambyses, the son of Cyrus the Great, in 522 B.C. Their coup was a failure, and the slaughter of the Magi that resulted in 521 is known to history as the Magophony. From Chaldea to Egypt and Greece, the survivors took their doctrine and organization. Egypt seems to have been the last great stronghold of Magism, and it was there that the Greek philosophers traveled to learn of the "mysteries."

Plato's writings are filled with allusions to the Egyptian teacher-priests; in the *Timaeus* we learn of Solon's journey there, and we know that Plato himself, as well as Pythagoras and Eudoxus, were initiated into the mystery religion. A Roman philosopher of later antiquity, Iamblichus, has preserved an account of the initiation rites, perhaps largely legendary if not wholly fictitious. According to Plato, however, the Egyptian priests knew of the founding of Athens itself, thousands of years before, and they also spoke of the sunken continent of Atlantis. A great testament to the power of an idea is the fact that Plato's story of Atlantis in the *Timaeus* and the *Critias* is the *only* source of that legend (other than the oracular pronouncements of Edgar Cayce within this century). These and other more secret facts were imparted only to those who survived the dreadful rites of initiation, and philosophers came from every part of the known world to study at the feet of the Egyptian Magi. Plato remained there thirteen years.

Magism and the legends veiling it in obscurity pervaded the whole of Greek philosophy and spread throughout the Roman Empire as Hellenist teachers wandered from city to city teaching and gaining disciples. But magic is a far more comprehensive phenomenon than can be confined to the vague history of secret orders; every nation and people has its own magic tradition, usually preserved in epic sagas and folklore as well as ancient practices. In Greece, necromancy, augury, dream-divination, and oracles were already ancient in the days of Homer. In Italy, especially in Rome, whose origin is shrouded in magical legend and myth, augury and sooth-saying were integral parts of religious observance. Throughout the Graeco-Roman world, the greater oracles and sibyls were revered and became the object of lengthy pilgrimages. Their fame endured well into the Christian era; one of them—the Cumean sibyl, Hierophila—was even believed to have prophesied the coming of Christ to the tyrant Tarquin in the third century B.C. This prophecy was renewed in the time of Augustus by the Tiburian sibyl, according to Christian legend. Thus the word "sibyl" appears in Christmas hymns to this day, and the phrase *"teste David cum sibylla"* of the grim "Dies Irae," the funeral sequence, refers to the dire predictions of Sambeth, daughter of Noah—one of the first of the sibyls, following legends favored by Justin Martyr, Clement of Alexandria, Origen, and Lactantius.

45

Three of the many oracles of Greece were particularly famous: that of Apollo at Delphi, of Zeus at Dodonna, and of Trophonius at Boetia. A woman prophet called the pythoness or pythia because of the presence (?) of snakes, which were associated with Apollo, perched herself on a tripod in the oracular temple, sometimes over a fuming gaseous vent or near a brazier of fuming laurel leaves, where she would reply to questions in cryptic, febrile tones which would then be interpreted by a priest. Often the deliberately enigmatic answers were less than favorably received, but their very ambiguity guaranteed that the oracle was always right. But occasionally the prophetess was less than indirect in her answers; Nero had the Delphic priest mutilated and the pythia buried alive after she accused him (rightly) of matricide.

These oracles and sibyls of antiquity raise the question of natural prophecy, to which we shall return in due time. At this point, it is sufficient to recall that magic permeated classical culture from philosophy and theology to the everyday matters of household chores and farming. Oracular utterances were held in great esteem by the simple folk of villages and the countryside as well as by the nobility and emperors. Necromancers, sorcerers, sibyls, and pythonesses were all mouthpieces of the supernatural world who portended the future or divined the present through words and signs. But like the prophets of Israel, they and the Magi as well were independent of official cult and often rival claimants for the religious allegiance of the people, delivering moral imperatives rather than directions for proper liturgical comportment.

From the mountains of Tibet to the forests of Gaul, magic was a shared feature of classical cultures. Consequently, a wonderworker such as the mysterious Apollonius of Tyana—prophet, Magus and teacher—could travel the whole of the Roman Empire and find himself at home in palaces and shepherds' huts. A contemporary of St. Paul, Apollonius was long considered the rival of Jesus because of his wisdom, fearlessness, disdain of wealth and pomp, and even his miracles of healing, exorcism, and raising the dead. Certainly, Christian claims would be measured against the feats of men like Apollonius, for supernatural events were no novelty in Rome, and, on the other hand, Christians had much to be wary of in preaching Christ, who could very easily have seemed like just another Oriental thaumaturge to the superstitious citizens of the Empire. Strangely, even though both Paul and Apollonius studied in Tarsus at about the same time, there is no indication in the accounts of either that they ever knew of each other's existence. Apollonius died in the year 96 of the Christian era, famous, respected, and feared.

Not all magicians and seers fared as well, and even Apollonius barely escaped death on more than one occasion for his pronouncements, criticizing even Nero and Domitian to their faces. But Roman emperors, alternately patronizing and condemning magicians, astrologers, and soothsayers, were no less ambivalent than other ancient potentates. For too often the Magus was drawn into courtly intrigues to his own ultimate undoing; the word "sorcerer" became at this time synonymous with "poisoner," a custom which survived for due reason for over a thousand years. Therefore we discover without surprise that wizards, sorcerers, and astrologers were expelled from Rome in 139 B.C. Augustus had two thousand magical texts burned in the streets; Tiberius and Claudius banished magicians (other than their own), while Nero and Caligula, who themselves dabbled in sorcery, had many executed, as did Vitellius and many later emperors. According to legend, Simon the Magician, a character from Acts 8, perished falling at the prayers of Peter from a tower from which he had promised Nero to fly. Perhaps the major cause for the harsh treatment of magicians by the emperors was the fear that the sorcery used at their command against personal enemies could be turned against themselves.

Magic in the Christian Era

As Christianity emerged from the catacombs into the light of a new glory, it inherited with the imperial purple the official schizophrenia regarding magic. In the Acts of the Apostles (chapters 8 and 13) we encounter two wily sorcerers, Simon (whose fate was described above) and Elymas, whose suspicions of Christianity were met with even greater hostility by Peter and Paul. The Book of Revelation excluded sorcerers from the Heavenly City along with dogs, fornicators, idolators, and murderers (Rev. 22, 15). But a few centuries later, Jerome found it possible to speak highly of "the philosophers, the astronomers, the astrologers, whose wisdom, so useful to mankind, is confirmed by dogma, explained by method, and verified by experience."

For the next thousand years, the occult sciences would be favored by churchmen, both bishops and pope, and even Protestant monarchs would have their court astrologers and paid alchemists no less than would the Catholics; Elizabeth I and Catherine de Medici both employed magicians whose names (including Dr. John Dee and Nostradamus) have been recorded by history. But also during the fifteen centuries after Jerome's appraisal, wizardry, witchcraft, and divination would be outlawed for the masses, leading to the horrible extremes of the Catholic Inquisition and the witch hunts of Protestant Germany, England, Scotland, and America. A double standard was being deeply imbedded in the European attitude to magic, and we cannot discount the overwhelming evidence of the development of sheer hypocrisy during that millennium.

Paganism and Christian Magic

As the strength of the Christian Church waxed greater in the declining years of the Empire, pagan sorcerers were often anathematized along with the thaumaturgic societies which they initiated—the writings of the Greek Fathers, especially John Chrysostomos, reek with hostility. Civil laws were also passed against practitioners of the ancient arts. The crafty Emperor Valens in 373 sentenced to immediate execution all apprehended Magi, soothsayers, diviners, and, significantly, philosophers. Further legislation by Theodosius in 385 and 391 renewed the ban under penalty of death. Such laws, imposed by those who themselves employed sorcery and divination to scale the bloody ladder of ambition, followed the "apostasy" of the Emperor Julian, who abjured Christianity and attempted to reestablish polytheism and himself practiced magical rites.

Polytheism and magic did not expire with Julian and his official sorcerers; they simply took to the underground sanctuary of secret societies as had Christianity three hundred years before, and there the old rites survived, safe from the persecutions of half-Christian monarchs. In the marches, the situation was more humane and reasonable. In Gaul the Salic Laws of 424 imposed a fine of 2500 deniers on a convicted magician, but trebled the fine for a false accusation against a "free" woman, suggesting that the objects of suspicion were often the former priestesses of the old religions, a hint of the witchcraft mania of later centuries.

A long and bloody chapter in European history thus begins with the spread of Christianity across the lands of the *pagani,* where entire tribes were assimilated into the new religion often by virtue of conquest or the conversion of their leader: *cuius regio, eius religio.* But like the ancient priests and magicians of Rome the worshippers of the Saxon and Druid gods did not simply disappear, and often the gods themselves were merely "baptized": St. Michael becoming a favorite pseudonym for Mercury or Wodin, and St. Mary the Mother of God easily replacing Ceres, Venus, Vesta, or Freya. Guardian angels, patron saints, holy water and incense, sacred bread and wine—all were familiar enough to the semi-barbarian tribes encountered by the missionaries and armies of the Christian Empire. Theodosius's troops were hard pressed to discover the last sanctuaries of heathen worship in the great scouring of 426 simply because they overlooked the newest Christian shrines.

Even where Christianity took deep root, memories of former ways remained alive in custom and folklore, and the Church itself pursued a policy of conscious accommodation whenever possible. To this day the English names of half the days of the week honor Tiw, Wodin, Thor, and Freya, and the rest refer to planetary gods—the sun, moon, and Saturn. Hanging mistletoe is, of course, a Druid new year hangover. Easter and Christmas, Hallowmas and Candlemas were deliberately assigned to dates already hallowed by pagan religion.

Legends grew abundantly in that gloaming of ancient classical culture called the Dark Ages by later historians and these tales eventually matured into pervasive beliefs in witchcraft, sorcery, devil-worship, and were-animals throughout Europe. Of all the figures that haunt the shadows of those times of Europe's youth none is more fascinating than the great wizard of Arthurian lore, Merlin—the architect of Great Britain. Half-demon, half-saint, this strange character, who quite probably really lived in fifth-century Wales, came to represent for the medieval chronicler Geoffrey of Monmouth, and through him practically all Western civilization, the archetypical magician of antiquity. It is certainly against Merlin's memory that the stories of later alchemists and astrologers, wizards and thaumaturgists were created, for anyone who delved into the secrets of nature and the treasury of ancient wisdom "must" have been a sorcerer.

The emerging belief in witchcraft soon obscured the distinct role of the wizard as apocalyptic fears beginning in the early Middle Ages fanned the superstitious spark that eventually engulfed the whole of Europe in a centuries-long conflagration. But although the magician was eclipsed by the witch in popular belief, astrologers, diviners, and sorcerers still figured prominently in the affairs of royal houses, and thus subsidized were enabled to continue their search for wisdom and power. Alchemy in particular was the work of medieval magicians, and the alchemical quest for the Philosopher's Stone and the Elixir of Life perdured into the late Renaissance, laying the groundwork for the modern science of chemistry. Of course, the alchemist's knowledge of herbs and liquors made him a valuable dispenser of potions and poisons for those who could pay, and, having invested fortunes in equipment and experiments, many alchemists were eager to supplement their income.

A gradual change had been at work in the conception of magic, however, between the end of the Empire and the flowering of medieval Christendom. The Magus, a creature of classical culture, declined with it, leaving in large part only a memory attached to men such as Merlin or to the antics of clowns and imposters. The associates of Julian the Apostate, Maximus and Priscus, were perhaps the last of the great masters of ancient magic and they paid for it with their lives. Thereafter the mantle fell on the thin shoulders of charlatans and schemers anxious to gain power by currying the patronage of the mighty. When not eking out a living performing stunts, wart-charming, or fortune-telling, these degenerate Magi sold their knowledge: Louis XI of France, for instance, employed the Abbé Faure de Versois to dispose of his brother, the Duc de Guyenne, which the latter did by poison in 1472. In 1315 Hugh Geraud, Bishop of Cahors, had attempted to dispose of Pope John XXII in similar fashion; he was flayed alive for his efforts. The clergy were often involved in such plots, for they had access to libraries and the rudiments of education; Shakespeare's bungling Friar Lawrence is a typical instance, inadvertently bringing tragedy to the star-cross't Romeo and Juliet.

Belief in magic nevertheless flourished in the form of myriad superstitions, talismans, curses and blessings, cures and divining. For peasants, shopkeepers, guildsmen, soldiers, the clergy and nobility, the decrees of destiny and the mechanics of magic were at work in the most ordinary concerns of life. In the face of such rampant gullibility, the Church (anxious to protect its own monopoly on the supernatural) and the State often took official action against popular examples of magic, especially witchcraft and devil-worship. Nevertheless, it was not always a matter of jealousy or expedience; great and humane churchmen sought to discourage magical practices by exhortation and education. Augustine had opposed pagan thaumaturgy in his *City of God* as an affront to the miracles of simple faith. In the middle of the seventh century, Isodore of Seville attributed magic to human malice, urging pious Christians to avoid it. In 690 Theodore of Canterbury forbade satanism, divination, magic, and the donning of animal skins. In Germany, St. Boniface (who died in 794) required his converts to renounce belief in incantations, divination, witches, and werewolves.

Soon, however, as Christianity was made the official religion of the new empire, the urgings of preachers and missionaries gave way to laws and proscriptions. Banishment, scourging, and divers penalties short of death were imposed with increasing frequency in the last years of the first millennium, especially as the belief in witchcraft began to spread its baneful influence over Europe.

Magicians and Their Black Books

In attempting to identify the magicians of any epoch, one need not look far: anyone with more than ordinary (that is, minimal) wit or schooling was bound to have been considered a sorcerer at one time or other. The first of the Magi, as we have seen, was reputed to have been the grandson of Adam, Hermes-Thoth-Mercury. After the Great Flood, the first of the "new" magicians (other than the Magi of Mount Victory, who had weathered the storm) was Cham-Zoroaster, according to legend, whose identification with the founder of Mithraism is no coincidence. With Persian Zoastrianism began the dualism that would later give rise to black magic, satanism, and the witchcraft frenzy, for that religion was to influence both Manichaeism and the Waldensian heretics, and its memory survives even today in the valleys of Southern Europe. In twelfth-century Egypt, Moses encountered magicians later named Iannes and Iambres.

Biblical literature abounds with references to sorcerers and magicians of the Middle East. Solomon is considered in all later magical writings to have been the arch-magician of them all; the wicked King Manasseh also did more than dabble in sorcery (2 Kings 21, 6). Among the Greeks, Herodotus testifies to the existence of the Magi in his *History of the Persian Wars,* and Zenophon did not hesitate to call Socrates a magician. Plato, as we have seen, studied Egyptian magic. From the dimmer past, Homer's *Iliad* and *Odyssey* are filled with references to magic and witchcraft, with Circe and the necromancer Tiresias becoming favorite characters of later commentators, notably Dante. In legends of other peoples, from China to the Finnish *Kalevala,* similar magicians fill the pages of literature. In the classical Western tradition some of the more outstanding magicians include Berosus of Cos, Adamantius, Apollonius of Tyana, Mary the Jewess (a lady alchemist of the fourth century A.D.), Merlin, Prester John, Albertus Magnus, Roger Bacon, Robert Grosseteste, Arnauld of Villanova, Paracelsus, Cornelius Agrippa, and later, John Dee, Nostradamus, Cardinal Richelieu, Casanova, and Elias Ashmole, the founder of Freemasonry. Among the popes, Leo the Great, Honorius III, Sylvester II, Benedict IX, Gregory VI, Gregory VII (Hildebrand), John XX, and Sixtus V were considered magicians or sorcerers.

Whether or not all or any of these historical personages were actual magicians is of less significance than the fact that they were considered to have been by later generations. Many of the grimoires, the magical textbooks, were ascribed to them, and in particular to Solomon and Albertus Magnus. These "Negromantick Bookes" (called *grimoria* in Latin) number into the hundreds, but the most famous of them are the *Grimorium Verum*, the *Book of the Marvels of the World* (attributed to Albert), the *Grimoire of Honorius III* (and very grim indeed), the *Clavicle* (or *Key*) *of Solomon*, the *Lemegeton* or *Lesser Key of Solomon*, the *Testament of Solomon*, Johann Faustus's *Great and Powerful Sea Ghost, Hell's Coercion*, the *Little Albert*, and *The Red Dragon*. Most of the manuals were probably burned by the Inquisition and by witch hunters of England and Scotland, but many have survived and are found in museums the world over. A few turned up in the interesting hands of later sorcerers.

Modern Magi

During the infrequent lulls in the witch hunts and after the fires of the Inquisition had been banked for ever, the magician was to reappear in human society, not as the imposing and venerable scion of Apollonius, but a professional prophet, courtier, and showman. Men such as Michel Nostradamus, Cagliostro, the Count of St. Germain, often possessed real genius mixed with evident legerdemain.'

A hundred years later, the great sorcerers of the Victorian era appear—Eliphas Levi (died in 1875), Macgregor Mathers (died 1918), and the incredible, brilliant, outrageous Aleister Crowley, the last of the breed, who died in 1947. In these men, however, the various currents of Magism, witchcraft, black magic, and satanism, even alchemy, had blended to form a new creature. Gone was the pointed cap and starry gown, replaced by the silken robes of the parlor and the business suit. The old services of curing, charming, and removing hexes, which had been the wizard's humble duty to the simple folk, were now in the hands of "cunning men" and white witches, village healers, and "wise women."

Since the eighteenth century, magic has rarely appeared in "pure" form, and today most people are little aware that the word refers to anything other than theatrical prestidigitation and simple tricks. The witchcraft mania effectively eclipsed the more servile arts of thief-divination, finding lost or stolen property, healing by incantations and herbs, charming animals, and other functions of the folk-wizard. Even these services were overshadowed in village life by the cunning man or witch-doctor's more grisly function of pointing out witches and combatting their hexes, even to their destruction. Such occupational rites still characterize the witch-doctors of contemporary Africa, the South Pacific, and parts of sub-equatorial America. Differentiating between these "white" witches and their chief enemies, the hated, secret "black" witches—never an easy matter for the outsider—has been rendered almost impossible by the contamination of tradition by the importation of half-remembered tales of English country life of centuries past.

In England herself, the old cunning man, the village witch-doctor, has forever disappeared, the last members of that ancient caste being (it is believed) James Murrell of Hadleigh, South Essex, and George Pickingill of the witch-obsessed village of Canewdon. The cunning Murrell died in 1860, Pickingill in 1909, and with them perished an ancient tradition and lore that was begotten in the remote past of Druid Britain. But the sophisticated admirers of Mathers and Crowley still walk the parks of London and New York, and witchcraft itself has hardly vanished from either rural or urban life. That, we shall discover, is another story.

Magic has occupied a position of social invisibility since the rise of Western Christendom, but it has never budged from that throne of power no matter how strenuously its enemies sought to eradicate it, for the magical mentality is a deeply human note. It is capable of assuming numerous identities, each a careful approximation of the cultural visage itself. Therefore, magicians have shared the characteristics of their times, and often reflected unwittingly the dominant motifs of society, which time merely transforms.

Magicians of old, with exceptions such as Apollonius, were not only far removed from the lives of simple folk, whom they nevertheless aided on occasion; they were also almost invariably members of a secret society. This feature later inspired Eliphas Levi, Mathers, and Crowley to establish secret organizations in Victorian times (as classical architecture was similarly vulgarized). The penchant for forming such clubs resulted in the macabre but comical "War of the Sorcerers" that raged from 1887 to 1893, as two French societies of rival magicians hurled curses like bombshells between Paris and Lyons. Many of the combatants actually died during this series of metaphysical exchanges, which each hostile group attributed to the machinations of the opposition. The most famous of all magical societies was the English "Order of the Golden Dawn," which included not only Mathers and Crowley (who was later expelled) but also W. B. Yeats, Sir Bulwer Lytton (author of *The Last Days of Pompeii*), the Irish novelist Bram Stoker, whose gothic masterpiece *Dracula* is still a best seller, and the master occultist A. E. Waite. Crowley later founded his own Order of the Silver Star, which never came to much, and the Order of the Golden Dawn eventually petered out as well, having left a vivid mark on English literature. Despite a recent resurgence of interest in the writings of these nineteenth-century magicians, it is mainly limited to the confines of witch covens, satanist churches, and gnostic schools.

Magic is the response of the child within us all to the mysteries of human existence which demand an explanation of some kind—whether rational or not. We find assurance in learning or being told that we are not victims of chance in a universe of random events and ultimate chaos. The desire to know is servant to the need for assurance. In contemplating the riddle of existence and the awesome mysteries of the nocturnal sky, man, in quest of assurances and explanations, developed the most ancient of all sciences, to which we shall now turn our inquiries: astrology.

4.

Astrology—The Once and Future Thing

HAIR's "Aquarius" meant little enough in technical terms to the millions of teenagers who adopted it as a sort of national anthem of pop culture except that it implied that celestial mechanics would somehow assure that the future would be better than the past and certainly an improvement on the present:

> *When the moon is in the seventh house*
> *And Jupiter aligns with Mars*
> *Then peace will guide the planets*
> *And love will steer the stars.*
>
> *This is the dawning of*
> *The Age of Aquarius . . .*
>
> *Harmony and understanding*
> *Sympathy and trust abounding*
> *No more falsehoods or derisions*
> *Golden living dreams of visions*
> *Mystic crystal revelation*
> *And the mind's true liberation.*[1]

As the astrological dimension of the occult revolution became more a feature of everyday life, the lyrics from *Hair* took on a deeper significance, the realization that with the end of the world of Pisces, not only the era of Christendom but the whole of Western civilization was on the brink of total transformation.

As if deliberately pre-empting *Hair*'s prophetic anticipation of a happier tomorrow, Herman Kahn, and Anthony Wiener of

[1] Ragni and Rado, *Hair,* pages 2–3.

the Hudson Institute (hardly an oracle of the counter culture) published their master-plan for a technocratic future, *The Year 2000.* The battle of futurology was just beginning, however; in England, Stanley Kubrick was beginning production of the epic *2001: A Space Odyssey,* a definitely apocalyptic celebration of the death and resurrection of technological man amid the outer planets. The allusion to the Homeric poem was no accident—Homer was for the Greeks of old not only a bard but a prophet; the *Iliad* and the *Odyssey* were supremely religious books.

Arthur C. Clarke, Kubrick's collaborator on *2001,* was already enjoying a revival of some of his earlier science-fiction explorations of possible human futures such as in his wistful, brilliant *Childhood's End.* At the same time, Marshall McLuhan was still making pregnant asides about the super-consciousness of the human race now attainable through modern communications media, to the outrage of practically everyone but the budding counter culturalists. Teilhard de Chardin's cryptic philosophy of human potential and the Omega Point was still in the academic air, and there were not a few small altars built to the priest's memory in apartments and basement lounges. Chardin's eschatological expectations of the future of man were mirrored back to a mythical past in J. R. R. Tolkien's *The Lord of the Rings* trilogy, a thinly veiled apocalypse which became an immediate sensation on college campuses after a twenty-year "cooling off" period. Within two years, *Future Shock* would go to press.

As if on cue, a revolution of rising expectations about the future of the human race—as well as its sticky present—broke onto the American and European social scene with a brandishing of astrological charts, talk of "vibrations," extrasensory perception, the coming End of the World—all deeply rooted in old and new mythological interpretations of the changing of ages. Astrology had made a dramatic entrance on the stage of history.

Of all the varieties of testament to the change of aeons, *2001* is probably the most phenomenal. It became an instant success, symbolically catalyzing the fears and expectations of almost everyone, from the most ardent technocrat to the stonedest flower child, thousands of whom would drop acid or puff pot prior to spending night after night in the front row of theaters all across America—or even stretching out on the carpet under the panoramic screen, gazing up happily at the psychedelic colors and fluid forms that occupy a sizable portion of the film's climax.

Perhaps most American viewers identified the great black monolithic sentinels as "some kind of religious symbol." The feelings of awe and wonder that most viewers experienced in *2001* the first two or three viewings were not inappropriate: the film is a profoundly religious adventure—not because of the symbolism (there being very little) but because of the subject matter and the way it was treated, particularly in the case of the soundtrack music. Kubrick was playing with the viewer, creating a great cosmic joke, taking him for a ride—literally putting him right up *there* with the hapless astronauts: among the planets, at the mercy of powers absolutely beyond his control —a berserk computer on one hand (surely the twentieth-century equivalent of one of the Four Horsemen of the Apocalypse) and, on the other, a superhuman agency that manipulates space and time. The viewer's religious nerves tingled not because Kubrick was dealing with God, but because he was not. He was playing with astrology—the ancient, deeply rooted belief that human destiny is somehow identifiable with the stars and planets. Such matters are religious feelings. The religious element of *2001* was merely the thought of infinite space and superhuman intelligence mediated through an astrological filter.

Kubrick had it all there—evolution, extraterrestial life forms, technological finesse, believable space vehicles, a moon that looked like the moon ought to look, and enough conjunctions, oppositions, planetary transits, and astral influences to make the oldest astrologer reach for his ephemeris and protractor. (He admits that the only time he knowingly departed from scientific accuracy was in order to achieve a *magical* conjunction of the planets.) To be sure, 2001 never directly even approached astrology other than photographically, yet it pervades the film, not only in the mystique of the outer planets and their tutelary "spirits," but in the very manner of treatment, Kubrick's—and Clarke's—whole attitude to the cosmos.

Placing the next development in man at the end of this century is also a thoroughly astrological touch, and that is why 2001 is a visual variation on the themes of *Hair*. Both are humanist apocalypses, and anyone who does not yet realize that humanism is a religion has misunderstood a great deal of what the twentieth century is all about. Man-in-space is a religious event for Western civilization, whether astronauts read the creation story from Genesis or notch the butts of their spaceguns for another god who bit the stardust. The Russian cosmonaut's attempted witticism about not finding God "up here" was a fascinating admission that the Soviets, too, still associate the dark reaches of space with primitive religious feelings.

Archaic man dealt with the religious feelings of awe and terror evoked in him by the spectacle of the night sky by often worshipping the stars and planets. In his quest for religious certainty, contemporary man, if unable to adore what he knows are thermonuclear events and lifeless globules becoming a technician's junkyard, can nonetheless pay his respects by consulting an astrologer or perhaps just the daily horoscope in the newspaper. From a behavioral viewpoint, at least, astrology is a religion for millions of Americans and matters significantly in the religious world of most of this planet's four billion people. For although Western man may pretend that his astrological beliefs are scientifically based (which he might be surprised to learn is partially true), his motivation is strictly religious: he is searching for meaning in the cosmos and significance in his own life.

Among the young, most of the ardently astrological were formerly practicing Catholics or Protestants of conservative stripe who have dropped out of the "organized" church. (Though, on the other hand, many seem to be making the best of both worlds.) Astrological writers have unabashedly expounded the religious significance of belief in the influence of the stars; Carroll Righter and Jeane Dixon are both devout Christians, and Marc Edmund Jones, the dean of modern American astrologers, was a Presbyterian minister. But the virtual resurrection of astrological belief from the graveyard of medieval superstition and its portent of the emergence of a counter culture: an indictment of organized religion and the technological society.

The Architecture of the Universe

Like the magical view of life from which it sprang, astrology's archaic origins are lost in the aboriginal mists of time. It was already a developed body of knowledge and doctrine—a science, in other words—when the Sumerians began writing their grocery lists in cuneiform. At least five or six thousand years old, astrology is mankind's oldest science, perhaps as antique as magic and religion.

In legends of the Near East, astrology (like most everything else) was begun by Hermes Trismegistos, the founder of Magism. Apparently, astrology originated in Chaldea and became the spoil of conquering nations succeeding each other through the internecine years of ancient Mesopotamia: Babylonia, Assyria, and Persia, whence it passed into Egypt, Greece, and the mainstream of Oriental and Western culture. In the Far East, astrology had an equally ancient origin among the Indians and Chinese, and it appeared in parallel but independent fashion in pre-Colombian Mexico and more southern lands where the Mayan and Inca peoples lived. Giorgio di Santillana and Hertha von Dechend have traced the lineage of astrological lore in such a cross-cultural ambiance back to its earliest stages of development; their work, *Hamlet's Mill,* has already become a classic among historians and philosophers of science since its publication in 1969, and it is (again) no accident that the figure of Hamlet in his manifold guises wanders in and out of the narrative.

Mankind's fascination with stars, planets, and the two "nearer" celestial bodies is, then, far older and more fundamental than civilization itself. Far above the unforeseeable dangers of primitive life, the unchanging, incredibly orderly procession across the black vault of the heavens must have filled the aboriginal heart with admiration and longing. Such a mood is poignantly re-created in *2001*—the night-bound earth is a place of fearsome, lurking predators, of sudden screams of mortal terror which blaze in the dark silence like a comet flashing unexpectedly overhead. Only with daylight comes respite from fear and the possibility of food-gathering or hunting the hunter.

Discovering the use of fire would have had an impact on the magical world-view of dawn-man far greater than his invention of weapons or tools, because by capturing the light and heat of the sun something of the daytime could be preserved through nightfall, a psychological as well as physical blessing. Even when the moon was hidden there could be light—chaos was not totally in command of the dark-time. Early man was well aware of the consequences of his "theft" of fire, as the legends of Prometheus and Phaeton attest. He had crossed the threshold of immortality, risking the jealous vengeance of the gods. Phaeton, son of Helios, was hurled from his erratic, destructive course in the sun-chariot by one of Zeus's thunderbolts; for his philanthropic larceny, Prometheus was horribly punished, being chained to a rock where his liver was perpetually rent by a raven until he was liberated by Hercules and the sacrificial death of Chiron—mythological reminders that man himself was literally playing with fiery powers beyond his ability to control.

As ages passed, the pageant of the sky continued unvaryingly, save for the annual progress of the sun from north to south. But the winter's cold night never captured the sun, which returned each year after the winter solstice, bringing warm springtime and the miraculous rebirth of plant and animal life. Strange occurrences sometimes threatened the harmony of the heavens, however: eclipses of the sun and moon, the appearance of meteors and comets, the even rarer star-bursts still called *supernovae*. But none of these events, no matter how ominous, succeeded in altering the over-all serene and harmonious spectacle of the sky, which became the ideal of all peace and order.

Centuries of agricultural experience taught primitive man that the sun ruled the growing seasons and that the moon, too, governed the times for planting and harvesting as well as regulating the tides. Crude calendars were created—the return of the seasons marking the course of the year, during which the sun rose and set some 360 times, while the moon waxed and waned through thirteen periods. The "fixed" stars likewise returned to the same positions once each year, and the planets, despite their wandering, were also discovered to obey regular laws. The seasons, the tides, the migrations and hibernations of animals, the world and everything in it seemed to correspond to the turnings ("revolutions" in the strict sense) of the celestial bodies in space and time. Such observations, coupled with the immemorial feelings of awe, wonder, and night-terror, produced a primitive science and a religion as well. For men believed that the stars, the sun and moon, and the wandering lights were alive (for they moved) and divinely intelligent, as must indeed be true of those engaged in such consistent and powerful rituals. Further, like ghosts and demons and more friendly spirits, the sky-gods were susceptible of entreaty and vulnerable to attack. The sun must be helped in his battle with the great "dragon" that attempted to devour him periodically; he had to be coaxed not to depart forever at the winter solstice; he was besought for his benevolent rays and placated lest he scorch the crops.

In the gentle plains of Chaldea, astrology was developed further as enormous observatories called *ziggurats* were constructed, some over thirty stories high, on top of which priests studied and measured celestial phenomena. The ziggurat of the city of Babylon is believed to have been the prototype of the Tower of Babel of Hebrew tradition (Gen. 11, 1–10), an attempt to scale the very throne of heaven and therefore a sacrilege to the ancient Jews. England's famed Stonehenge (attributed to Merlin in later legends) was in all probability a similar and complicated astronomical observatory-computer, and the Mayan pyramids (as well as the Egyptian) fulfilled the same functions.

The Magi of Akkadia and Sumer, of Ur and Uruk, developed a coherent account that incorporated all the manifest features of archaic cosmology that became the basis of Western astrology and astronomy. Shamash the Sun-god and Sin the Moon-god (both male divinities) ruled the day and night. But their daily and yearly journeys never took them beyond a measurable distance from a central path (the "Way of Anu"), the heavenly equator which passed through the domain of thirty-six other lights, slower-moving stars which became the "counsellor gods" of Shamash and Sin. Each of these in turn was surrounded by lesser stars, over which they ruled as chiefs. Such constellations were called *berou*, and were imagined to be outlines of animals and fabulous creatures of ancient legends and myths such as the *Enuma Elish*, the Babylonian Genesis. (The authors of *Hamlet's Mill* contend [with Plato] that the great myths of all peoples were codifications of astrological doctrine in a form of oral shorthand, by which celestial events could be described and transmitted to future generations without reliance on yet cumbersome forms of writing. A great deal of evidence has been amassed to support this theory.) Some of these animal forms are familiar to us today: the goat-fish (Capricorn), the Scorpion, the Lion, and the Bull, and we still call the constellations of the entire sky by their ancient names. The Greeks called the twelve constellations of the celestial equator the *zodiac,* "the parade of animals," by which name we also know it today.

The ancient observers were aware of other inhabitants of the northern and southern limits of the zodiac, which borders were called the "Ways" of Enlil and Ea (corresponding to our Tropics of Cancer and Capricorn). These they named *bibbus* or "wild goats," irregularly moving lights the Greeks would call *planetoi,* "wanderers." These became the interpreters of Shamash and Sin, and each was considered the abode of a god. Five of these planets were known in antiquity—the others not being discovered until the last two centuries. Their names, with Greek and Latin equivalents, are as follows, beginning with the sun and moon (the earth, not then considered a planet, but the center of the whole panorama—which it is, phenomenologically—was called Ea by the Chaldeans, Gaia by the Greeks, and Terra by the Romans):

Shamash	– Helios	– Sol
Sin	– Selene	– Luna
Nabu	– Hermes	– Mercury
(or Nebo)		
Nergal	– Ares	– Mars
Ishtar	– Aphrodite	– Venus
Marduk	– Zeus	– Jupiter
Ninurta	– Kronos	– Saturn
(or Ninib)		

Divided into weeks of seven days, the lunar month was also parcelled out to gods, which is the origin of the names of the days of the week to the present.

This early scientific-religious attempt to classify, measure, and tabulate the celestial environment also gave rise to ancient mathematics, particularly geometry, which was an impressive achievement. As astrologer of the school of Sippar, for instance, calculated the lunar month to be twenty-nine days, twelve hours, forty-four minutes, and thirty-three seconds, erring by a meager .6 of a second. The Chaldeans, millenniums before Christ, divided the year into 365¼ days, and although they employed double hours to divide the day—corresponding to the twelve *berou*—each hour was divided into sixty minutes and 360 seconds. Our clocks are divided exactly the same way, including the use of twelve hours rather than twenty-four. Arithmetic, geometry, and trigonometry, despite their Greek names, were invented by the Chaldeans. The Greek influence is traceable to Berosus of Cos, a Babylonian priest of the fourth century B.C., who imported into that country the whole body of Chaldean astrology, mathematics, and religion.

From a religious viewpoint, the emergence of astrology not only established the worship of celestial divinities throughout the known world, but determined the character of the Judaeo-Christian cosmogony as well. Besides wholesale borrowings from their neighbors, the Jews developed their monotheistic religion in conscious reaction to Mesopotamian cult and belief. For the Hebrews, at least in the latter centuries B.C., the Lord God *created* the stars, planets, sun, and moon. They were not gods. Even foreigners' observatories and their staffs were condemned outright. From the Tower of Babel to the diatribes of Isaiah and Ezekiel, a current of anti-astrological bias runs like a symphonic theme.

The deliberate demythologization program of the Jews created much of the unique character of ancient Judaism, even despite the inevitable accretions from the originally detestable sources. To be sure, much later, during the intertestamental period, apocalyptic writings unconsciously incorporated a large measure of Greek thought, including astrological themes, which were combined with Persian dualism into a syncretistic, highly symbolic genre of religious literature. Apocalyptic writing, such as parts of Daniel, the Books of Enoch, and others, had a lasting impact on both later Judaism and Christianity. By the end of the first millennium of the Christian era, cabalism and astrology were

bring myth or story down to scientific fact

67

imbedded deeply in all the religions of the Western world, from Islamic Egypt to the coasts of Ireland. Much of the eschatological, apocalyptic aura of contemporary astrology owes its origin to the melting pot of the Near East, when the ancient empires and religions clashed and interpenetrated each other in the sprawl of Roman dominion.

The Royal Art

Ancient astrology was vastly different from that which passes for "star messages" among believers today. It was known in Chaldea as the "royal art," not because astrologers were kings (later Christian traditions about Matthew's Magi notwithstanding), but for the reason that birth charts and horoscopes were "erected" only for the royal household. The destiny of the king and his family was what mattered most, for not only did royalty embody the state, but the king paid the astrologers and subsidized the observatories. Little by little, however, astrology was democratized under the aegis of Greece, for every man was, after all, a child of the stars. The magical world of antiquity, shared by nobles and serfs alike, disposed them to accept wholesale the entire corpus of Chaldean lore.

All astrology is based on magical principles, despite its reliance on observation. The first principle is aptly summarized by the Hermetic axiom: As above, so below. This, of course, presupposes the essential unity of all reality with the myriad interconnections of multiform manifestations known only to the adept. Not only were the rise and fall of kingdoms foretold in the stars, but earthy disasters and catastrophes fell under their sway—both words contain the Greek "aster," "star," within them. Solar and lunar eclipses were omens as were comets and novae. Events on earth merely fulfilled what occurred first in the heavens.

Man became the central focus of the intervalent connections

between earth and heaven, a "microcosmic" replica of the "macrocosm," his bodily organs being influenced by the planets and zodiacal signs. Lesser animals and planets were likewise related to the stars as miniature versions of the microcosmic human world. Thus animals had a kingdom presided over by the lion. Totemism fits well into such a scheme, or, more likely, this kind of astrological zoology probably represents a higher form of the totemic principle.

Astrology's second law is the inexorability of universal cause and effect, known in Hindu philosophy as *karma,* but present in all primitive thought. Archaic feeling that the perfect harmony of the cosmos, once disturbed, will inevitably reassert itself, that every action has its repercussions in space and time, become prime ethical principles as well as ontological axioms in true astrological thought.

Recently, an ecological awareness has gripped many in the Western world, especially the young, that resembles the fatalistic karma of Hindu and Western astrology. Not coincidentally, within the youth-oriented counter culture both astrology and ecology are well-favored, for both are based on a wholistic understanding of the interrelatedness of nature, and both share a moralistic bias. "As you sow, so shall you reap." As far back as the Middle Ages, comets were often associated in a reciprocal relationship with human history, and eclipses were as much omens of divine retribution as the product of human sinfulness. The American Protestant mystic Edgar Cayce claimed in trance that the same karmic consequences are involved in the appearance and effects of sunspots: "Then what are the Sun spots? A natural consequence of that turmoil which the sons of God in the earth reflect upon the same (the Sun) . . . [which are in turn responsible for] the disruptions of communications of all kinds."[2]

[2] Margaret H. Gammon, *Astrology and the Edgar Cayce Readings,* Virginia Beach, 1967, page 16.

We shall return to Cayce later. Here it is enough to note that the eschatological panic that has been spawned by ecological jeremiads is little different than feelings experienced in the past: "There will be signs in the sun and moon and stars, and upon the earth distress of nations bewildered by the roaring of sea and waves . . ." (Luke 21, 25).

Such a lone passage certainly does not prove that Jesus was an astrologer, but it at least points up the fact that eschatological thinking of whatever origin reflects a consistent tendency towards understanding history in relation to celestial events. Eschatology, as we might expect, being the theology of ultimate crisis, is a fundamental feature of true astrological systems. This became explicit with the discovery of an astronomical fact that shook the archaic world even more terribly than Galileo's heliocentrism.

The Great Year and the End of Time

By the third century B.C., it had become evident that the ancient belief in the eternal and immaculate perfection of the celestial revolutions was an illusion. Around 120 B.C., Hipparchus (who also rejected the Pythagorean notion that the earth was a sphere) blandly recorded that strange observation known as the precession of the equinoxes, a slow movement of the solar axis through all the constellations of the zodiac over a period of 25,920 years. The fact that the visible stellar revolutions were involved in a vastly slower, more cumbersome movement was apparently known long before, however; Hipparchus was merely repeating an ancient discovery and giving it a name.

Unknown, of course, to the ancients, the change in the positions of the fixed stars as a whole is caused by the tilt of the earth, the axis of which "prolonged to the celestial North Pole describes a circle around the North Pole of the [solar] ecliptic, the true 'center' of the planetary system, the radius of this circle being the same magnitude as the obliquity of the ecliptic with respect to the equator: $23\frac{1}{2}°$."[3] The same tilt accounts for the seasons, the earth's "wobble," and the gradual shifting of the Pole Star from place to place.

From the viewpoint of an earthbound observer, this rather complex situation would have been detected experientially as an unbelievably slow regression of the equinoxes through the signs of the zodiac. In other words, the constellation Aries, which for over a thousand years was "rising" on the eastern horizon at dawn on the morning of the vernal equinox, March 21, gradually gave way to the constellation Pisces. No doubt centuries of exact observation were required to detect so minute a differentiation in the position of a few stars, given the simple instruments of the ancients.

It is probably difficult for us to imagine the cold terror that must have gripped the archaic astrologers as they recognized the awful truth about the "eternally constant" sky: the stars were slipping out of place, thus threatening the entire cosmos with absolute disintegration. An echo of their terror exists in a fragment of a poem from Akkadia, the *Era-Epos,* in which Marduk exclaims:

> *When I stood up from my seat and let the flood break in,*
> *then the judgment of earth and heaven went out of joint . . .*
> *The gods, which trembled, the stars of heaven—*
> *their position changed, and I did not bring them back.*

This "tilting" of the earth and heaven is reflected in many myths of the ancient world which survived the even more fascinating cosmic reprieve that came in the form of a second discovery: the precession of the equinoxes was not a haphazard fracture, but a slow rotation of the entire vault of heaven, which took nearly 26,000 years to complete itself, restoring Aries to its ascendency. Hence a great "solar year" was formulated, and like the annual revolution of the sun, it was divided into twelve segments, one

[3] Santillana and von Dechend, *Hamlet's Mill,* Boston, 1969, page 325.

71

for each of the signs (constellations) of the zodiac, lasting approximately 2160 years apiece.

Consequently, the Age of Pisces is said to have begun around the end of the first century B.C., corresponding with the birth of Jesus, whose acronym, moreover, in Greek is *ichthus,* meaning "fish." Thus the fish became the symbol of the Christian Church. It is perhaps not without significance that the *shofar,* or ram's horn, played a symbolic role (and still does) in Hebrew religious ceremonies, for the age that was dedicated to Aries (the Ram) began with the trek of Abraham from the land of Chaldea.

We are now living, as we have learned from *Hair,* in the "dawning of the Age of Aquarius," but more immediately in the twilight of the Age of Pisces. Some astrologers believe that the coming Age actually started as early as 1962, when a major conjunction occurred in the constellation Aquarius in the month of February. At any rate, we seem indeed to be witnessing the decline of the era of material triumph of Christendom as well as the end of an historical period of earth's history, as we have seen. By chance, perhaps, the attributes of the Piscean Age, a melancholy period ruled by the brooding Neptune, are applied to Hamlet: "psychic, emotional, impressionable, prone to moods of loneliness and despondency, liable to sudden outbursts of severity which contrast strangely with his habitual gentleness. He is deeply religious, yet unrestrained in his flights of daring speculation . . ."[4] Aquarius, an "airy" sign (the twelve signs are divided into three sets or "triplicities" signified by air, fire, water, and earth), suggests that the coming age will be one of peace, brotherhood, scientific and humanitarian progress: the Age of the Holy Spirit, according to the symbolic interpretation of Carl Jung.

[4] Isabelle Pagan and Alan Leo, "The Twelve Signs of the Zodiac," in *The Coffee Table Book of Astrology,* Edited by John Lynch, New York, 1967, page 235.

We might set an arbitrary date for the inauguration of the Age of Aquarius as *2001*, give or take a few decades. Then, within the lifetime of most people now alive, mankind will enter a new era. Whether that will be a privilege or an ordeal depends upon the severity of the shock waves of cultural upheaval, for in the decline of the ages is foreordained the decline of its civilizations; Western civilization—if astrology's millennial wisdom can be trusted—is on the verge either of transformation or destruction. Thus the "end of the world" is a function of the precession of the equinoxes in a relative sense, which mythologically explains the eschatological expectations of Jesus' times and our own as well. The end is written in the signs of the sun and stars. And at some future time, the great solar year itself may come to an end, it is believed, in a great cosmic conflagration, perhaps only to begin all over again.

The Fall of Astrology

A second repercussion of the discovery of the precession of the equinoxes was the necessity of revising the character of the astrological zodiac itself, for each constellation was slowly drifting away from its previous location, thus invalidating all the complicated forecasts, interpretations, and the like. By Hipparchus's day, the lapse amounted to about thirty degrees: the equivalent of an entire sign; today, the rift has doubled. But systems are more resilient than men, and it was determined by various series of conclaves that no matter how the constellations might slide, the signs named for them would continue to occupy the ancient positions in relation to the months of the year. Thus two zodiacs were recognized, the sidereal band of constellations and the "tropical" set of equally divided signs. Such a state of affairs cast an unfavorable light on the whole enterprise, abetted by the ridicule of critics of the caliber of Cicero. Despite the loss

73

of faith, astrology continued in most people's minds to represent the very architecture of fate and cosmos as if nothing had ever happened, much less the threat of absolute chaos.

A third characteristic of astrological thinking was more firmly re-established by the resolution of the great solar year's disjunction from the ideal zodiac: time was henceforth to be understood as a great cycle as recurrent as the seasons but now as determinate, and as eternal as the existence of the cosmos itself, without beginning and without end.

Again, there was a notable exception from the cyclical view of time: the Jews, oppressed and often enslaved, had ample time to experience the astrological views of their captors. And for many reasons, they not only rejected the temptation to resign themselves to fate but looked forward more eagerly to the Day of the Lord, the ultimate vindication of their ancient faith in the Lord of both Cosmos and History, the God of Promise.

Early Christianity inherited this belief, and, as we have already hinted, Jesus himself was embued with eschatological fervor. His followers interpreted the Day of the Lord as Christ's return to judge the living and dead and thus inaugurate the eternal messianic era, the *parousia* or "presence." But even before Jesus' lifetime, belief in a concretely historical "judgment day" had begun to give way to a "spiritualized" interpretation: the kingdom lay beyond time in an eternal, transcendent realm. Repeated disappointments had resulted in an indefinite delay of God's vindication for the Jews, just as Christ's delay was prolonged and eventually postponed until some unknown future for Christians. This also helps to explain why Jesus' eschatological preaching had fired the national ambitions of the zealots to the extent that he had to reprove them for "politicizing" his teaching (at least as described by the evangelists).

Both Jewish and Christian eschatological expectations were eventually replaced in large measure by Neo-Platonic theories of eternal essences and temporal recurrence, and "that day" became more a myth than a hope. Thus, despite the inveighments of the rabbis and Christian Fathers, the way was prepared for the entrance of astrology into Judaeo-Christian theology, which by the early Middle Ages was an accomplished fact. The re-emergence of Greek thought and magical belief via their Arabian sojourn was the last step in the process.

For the medieval West, Claudius Ptolemy, an Alexandrian astrologer of the third century A.D., had supplied mankind with an eternally adequate schema of the cosmos, which even allowed for eccentricities of planetary orbits and retrograde motion. More and more holes punctured Ptolemy's theories but ever-resourceful scholars, loath to part with so masterful and beautiful a plan, applied cosmological mud-plasters, until the ancient science was a mélange of imaginary spheres, gears, and exceptions to rules.

Not everyone, of course, agreed with the dominant theories. Among astrology's detractors up to the Copernican revolution, when the scientific and artistic aspects of astrology parted company, we find truly gifted minds: Cicero, who rejected the whole business; Gregory of Nyssa, John Chrysostomos, Basil, Ambrose, and Augustine, among the Christian Fathers, whose opposition was aimed primarily at the magical elements; centuries later, Calvin, Jonathan Swift, and the later Agrippa inveighed against the art. Despite such enemies, astrology's adherents effectively dominated scientific and literary thought from the time of Augustus through the centuries when Plotinus, the Christian philosopher Boethius, the Sicilian priest Julius Firmicus Maternus (an astrologer), and Jerome were the architects of culture. By the time of Albertus Magnus, Roger Bacon, and Thomas Aquinas, when the Arabian influence was in its heyday, astrology and Ptolemy's universe were firmly entrenched in the teachings of the schools and the Church. Dante was a staunch believer, and for centuries even the popes subsidized court astrologers. The famous Johannes Campanus, whose method of house division is still favored, was in the service of Pope Urban IV, and on Campanus's death in 1297, Thomas Campanella, an ex-Dominican priest, succeeded to his position. Paracelsus was an astrological adept in the court of Hungary, while Catherine de Medici employed and consulted many magicians and astrologers, notably Nostradamus and Auger Ferrier. Dr. John Dee was an astrologer in the pay of Queen Elizabeth. Kepler, Brahe, Copernicus, Galileo, and Newton all accepted the basic principles. But the climate was indeed changing; Harvey ridiculed and investigated magical claims, and Galileo himself became more a debunker than a believer. During the witch-hunts of the seventeenth century, many astrologers avoided the stake solely because of royal favor. Others were simply too popular to burn; in 1651 William Lilly, an English public astrologer, foretold a great conflagration that would befall London—after the Great Fire of 1666, he was indicted on a charge of arson! Happily, he was acquitted.

But of course it is a matter of historical fact that the passing of Renaissance science from dawn to daylight doomed the old royal art to increasing disfavor although, like magic, it never completely lost its hold on the masses or the nobility. Even Napoleon is believed to have consulted the old priest-astrologer Pierre le Clerc. The middle nineteenth century witnessed the popularity of published astrological almanacs by Englishmen adopting the lofty names of Zadkiel, Raphael, and Sepharial. On the continent, astrology and magic enjoyed a rise in favor that increased as the century waned. Since then, both have had their fortunes fluctuate, ostensibly in inverse proportion to the state of natural harmony and international concord. Like the sale of ouija boards, astrology's popularity seems dependent on war, rumors of war, economic crises, and other calamities.

5.

The Celestial Machinery and How It Works

OUR familiar notion of astrology reflects a simple and rather simplified version of the varied applications it has enjoyed since its ancient origin in the Fertile Crescent. In the beginning were *natural* and *juridical* (or judicial) astrology, the latter being subdivided into mundane, genethliacal, horary, electional, physiognomical, medical, agricultural, and esoteric or occult varieties.

Natural astrology was originally the study and measurement of the movements of stars and planets within the zodiac, but not limited to it exclusively, which represents the prototype of modern astronomy and astrophysics and their source. Applying such observations to earthly events and interpreting the results of such comparisons was the royal art of judicial astrology, at first preoccupied with predicting earthquakes, tides, eclipses, floods, wars, the birth and death of kings, the rise and fall of their power, and similar affairs of national consequence. This kind of astrology still exists although it is rarely heard of: *mundane* astrology. Most of us are more familiar with *genethliacal* astrology, the ordinary birth-sign predictions of the daily papers, which also involves elements of *electional* astrology, which deals with matters of advice and volition, based on the daily shifts in celestial patterns. *Horary* astrology purports to answer questions of the moment, an achievement resting on casting horoscopes for singular matters such as occupation, marriage, business concerns, and the other agenda pertaining to *houses,* the twelve subdivisions of the sky-map corresponding somewhat to the signs of the zodiac.

Such employment of astrological technique easily degenerates into *astromancy* or fortune-telling by the stars, a practice which was strongly attacked by Christian theologians from Augustine to the present. The other forms of judicial astrology are either self-explanatory or too obscure and complicated to consider in detail. *Occult* astrology, however, differs from the others primarily in the esoteric nature of the interpretation, tending toward the mystical.

Common to all kinds of astrology are: the planets, with their changing positions and mutual aspects; the tropical signs of the zodiac, which correspond to the months and seasons; and the interpretation of all this in present or future context in terms of the traditional meaning and values of the whole assemblage. (The sun and moon are still considered planets by astrologers, although the satellites of other true planets have no importance.) Of course, things get much more complicated when the nodes of the moon, the *Pars Fortunae* or other "Arabian Points" and similar appurtenances, are brought to bear on the destiny of the "native," that is, the person whose birth-chart or other horoscope is under consideration.

The most common chart in use today (there are several) is a circle representing a map of the celestial environment seen edge-on, sort of a side-view of the solar system and the zodiac arranged around the earth, which is taken to be the center of the universe. (It makes little difference that it is not, really, for the distances between all the planets remain constant even as they revolve whether the earth or the sun occupies the middle position in the map; the traditional scheme thus possessing the merit of phenomenological neatness.)

The left side of the chart represents (more or less) the East, the line extending from the midpoint of the left semi-circle to the opposite point standing for the horizon. Temporally, the points of intersection are dawn and sunset, respectively. A line bisecting the horizon points "up" to the midheaven and down to the

immum coeli or undersky. Thus the horoscope ("view of the hour") is a spatio-temporal diagram, assuming a point of observation at the north looking south. The signs of the zodiac are arranged around the periphery of the circle in equal, thirty-degree arcs, traditionally divided again into thirds or decanates, so-called since each "decan" occupies ten degrees of the whole. The signs of the zodiac are movable, depending on the time of year; the "universal horoscope" places Aries, the sign of the vernal equinox, just below the eastern horizon, in the position of "ascendency." At any given time of year or day, the "ascendent" will vary, since the whole zodiac revolves around the earth once every twenty-four hours as well as once a year in terms of the sun's position. Thus, for an individual "native," it is necessary to know the exact moment of birth to determine the positions of the signs in his birth-chart.

The signs rotate in a clockwise direction spatially but counterclockwise temporally. Each sign, as we have seen, occupies exactly thirty degrees of space (unlike the constellations). Further dividing the sky-map spatially on the basis of the intersection of the ecliptic, the celestial equator or the "prime vertical" joining the zenith and nadir of the earth and twelve equal sections of the earth's spherical surface produces the "houses," whose dividing lines or "cusps" will vary trigonometrically depending on which of the three basic lines is chosen to cut the circles. The houses are traditionally unequal in size, although in recent centuries there has been a trend towards an equal-house method of division. Actually, seven different methods are commonly employed: those of Campanus, Regiomontanus, the Porphyrean, Morinus, and Placidean systems, the equal-house or Zenith system (favored by Jung), and the horizontal system.

The reason for assigning twelve houses is disputed, but it appears to have been the immemorial custom which is sufficient warrant for a traditional practice such as astrology. These, naturally, correspond easily to the signs of the zodiac, although unlike the signs, the houses are fixed ordinarily, perhaps being no more than subsections of the circular chart itself. Each of the houses regardless of how they are all divided, represents some area of life analogous to the influences of the planets and the signs. How all these interrelate and determine an over-all interpretation is settled by locating the position of the planets, sun, and moon in the houses in the general context of the signs. This is done by consulting an astronomical *ephemeris* or table of the planets' places according to the days of the year. Figures relating to the exact time of the native's birth, the location, and the year can be converted to Greenwich mean time and sidereal time and by the aid of logarithmic tables the location of the planets directly over the birthplace at the proper time can easily be ascertained, thus giving a relatively unique character to the chart. Someone born at the same time and place as the native would, of course, have the same birth-chart. Such persons are called "astral twins," and according to tradition such twins have a remarkably parallel life-history, examples of which can be found in the first chapter of Joseph Goodavage's *Astrology: The Space Age Science.* (A handy reference manual with all necessary tables for erecting a horoscope or birthchart can be found in *Astrology for Everyone* by Edward Lyndoe, one of England's more popular astrologers. Louis MacNeice's *Astrology* also contains the basic information necessary, plus a candid and delightfully written history of the royal art.)

Having determined the planet's places and once they have been inserted in the chart, the astrologer proceeds to interpret the horoscope in terms of the planetary aspects, the houses in which they fall, and the influence of the signs. For instance, each planet has a positive, neutral, or negative character: Jupiter (the Greater Fortune) and Venus (the Lesser Fortune) are "benefic" as is the sun; Mars and Saturn are malefic; the moon and Mercury are variable or neutral; whereas the three most recently discovered planets, Neptune, Uranus, and Pluto are more or less undetermined. A native's "fortune" depends on the relationships between the planets (aspects) and the houses they fall in and also rule. A scheme of the correspondences looks something like this:

Each sign corresponds also to one of the four ancient elements, which gives to the sign the quality of that element: fire, water, earth, or air. Dividing the twelve signs by the four elements gives us the *triplicities:* Aries-Leo-Sagittarius (fire); Taurus-Virgo-Capricorn (earth); Gemini-Libra-Aquarius (air); and Cancer-Scorpio-Pisces (water). Each member of the triplicity has "sympathy" with its own, a lesser compatibility with the next-in-line, and antipathy with the contraries: fire with water, for instance. These relationships are applications not only of alchemy but of the mutual aspects of the planets and signs: the major aspects are conjunction, opposition, trine, and square, depending on whether the two bodies (or signs) are 0°, 180°, 120°, and 90° apart in longitude. Trine (and its half, sextile or 60°) are considered favorable, square and opposition unfavorable or "afflicted." The

SIGN	SYMBOL	TIME	RULING PLANET	SYMBOL	HOUSE	INFLUENCES
Aries	♈	Mar. 21 Apr. 20	Mars	♂	I	Personal appearance; physical body; the self
Taurus	♉	Apr. 21 May 21	Venus	♀	II	Finance; possessions
Gemini	♊	May 22 June 21	Mercury	☿	III	Relation to surroundings; communications; short trips
Cancer	♋	June 22 July 22	Moon	☽	IV	Home life; inherited tendencies; the father
Leo	♌	July 23 Aug. 23	Sun	☉	V	Children; pleasure; love; display
Virgo	♍	Aug. 24 Sept. 23	Mercury	☿	VI	Domestic affairs; health; service
Libra	♎	Sept. 24 Oct. 23	Venus	♀	VII	Marriage; partnerships
Scorpio	♏	Oct. 24 Nov. 22	Mars (or Pluto)	♇	VIII	Death; inheritance; self-sacrifice; sexual expression
Sagittarius	♐	Nov. 23 Dec. 21	Jupiter	♃	IX	Science; philosophy; religion; long journeys
Capricorn	♑	Dec. 22 Jan. 20	Saturn	♄	X	Profession; fame; the mother
Aquarius	♒	Jan. 21 Feb. 19	Uranus (or Saturn)	♅	XI	Friends; hopes; group goals
Pisces	♓	Feb. 20 Mar. 20	Neptune (or Jupiter)	♆	XII	Fear; restrictions and confinements; enemies

reason for the varied influences of the aspects is buried in numerological mysticism, but it works out tidily enough. And there is more.

The first members of each of the triplicities are called *cardinal;* they are the hinges or most prominent influences; the next set (the second of each triplicity) are *fixed* signs—less apt to extreme outbursts; the last set are *mutable* and are more likely to vary than the others. This category is called "the *quadruplicities,*" only one of a multitude of signal subdivisions proposed through the ages. There are, as well, lesser aspects, Arabian points, and the whole marvelous interplay of planets in other planets' signs and houses, which produces *exaltation, detriment,* and *fall,* all of which bear mightily on the native's fate. If two planets are found in each other's signs, they are in "mutual reception," another weighty discovery. Sometimes a sign may be completely eclipsed by house cusps; it is then "intercepted."

Assigning planets, houses, signs, the ascendent; calculating influences and listing effects; all the measuring and checking—these are but the beginning, preliminary steps to *interpretation* the goal of all traditional astrology, which involves at least by implication the possibility of prediction. And while the general outlines of astrological lore are fairly consistent at least in the West, the details of interpretation are as varied as the biases of the practitioner and the tradition that he follows—and there are many. Further, even within the limits of consensus, all the paraphernalia of occultism can be summoned for a really thorough interpretation. For instance, in the cabala, the twelve tribes of Israel correspond to the twelve stones of the sacred ephod and to the zodiac. Each of the Tarot cards is also related to a zodiacal sign within the "circle of fate" of each major planet. Then there are the greater genii or archangels, with their opposing demons, for each planet and sign, each having a mystical significance, a name, and a part of the body to govern. Thus Hermanubis, the genius of Cancer, rules the chest, lungs, ribs, spleen, and disorders thereof. Thirty-six lesser but similar genii preside over the decanates. Each year is likewise governed by one of the seven planetary genii, each of whom has power for thirty-six years; thus the moon (ruled by Pi-Joh, also the Genius of the brain) governs from 1945 to 1980; the sun (under Pi-Re, Genius of the forehead) will take control from 1981 to 2016. The complications are endless; it is also possible, when in doubt, to resort to as many as ten trans-Plutonian planets for additional clarification.

Astrologers can also "progress" a chart by comparing it to charts drawn up to correspond to any given year well in advance. The sun, for instance, moves 1°1' each *year* from its original position on the date of birth, which happens to correspond to the sun's position the *day* after the birth date as well. By the implicit magical correspondence, therefore, one day of life can be considered equivalent to one year of life, so that a horoscope drawn up for the twenty-first *day* of a native's life supposedly indicates his fortune during his twenty-first *year* of life. Whether the astrologer uses one-degree-for-one-year or one-day-for-one-year (the two more common *transit* methods of progression), the results will be the same, for they are based on the simple fact of the sun's progress. There are at least fifty more ways of progressing a chart, all of which border on astromancy, and none of which needs detain us further.

All in all, traditional and especially occult astrology are indeed exact, whether they are sciences or arts. And very surely, the newspaper and television varieties of prediction are faint reflections of the "true" practice of the ancient tradition just outlined —so general as to be practically meaningless and yet the most popular form of astrology. This perhaps proves that mere complexity is not what makes for the fascination of astrology, but rather that it represents an alternative explanation for the events of life, whether fortune, accidents, or the absurdities that befall us.

Coincidentally, there have been several attempts in the recent past (considering the life-span of the royal art) to shed the cumbersome paraphernalia of antiquity in order to develop a more streamlined version. In Germany, the efforts of Reinhold Ebertin to establish the more respectable-sounding cosmobiology date back to 1932. Ebertin and his followers, many of whom are Americans, wish to dismantle the traditional houses, aspects, and anything more peripheral than planets and signs. The old-fashioned horoscope is replaced by a "cosmogram" with only three cusps. So far, cosmobiology has been unable to displace the traditional view of astrology in the affection of its devotees.

The American astrologer Dane Rudhyar, a disciple of Marc Edmund Jones, has, contrary to Ebertin's methodology, reduced the importance of the planets and deals mainly with the psychological interpretation of the birth sign and ascendent, emphasizing (with Jung) the traditional, archetypal significances. Rudhyar seems to be gaining an increased following, aided no doubt by the untechnical, deftly written articles and books which he has produced over the past two decades. Significantly, Rudhyar denies that there is any scientific (that is, physical) basis for astrology's validity. Rather, it is for him simply a cosmic personality theory based on thousands of years' observation.

Vastly different from either Rudhyar or Ebertin, although more closely resembling the latter, and totally opposite the high priests of popular astrology such as Carroll Righter, Zolar, Omarr, Cean, and Dion Fortune, America's sleeping prophet Edgar Cayce enunciated a fascinating astrological doctrine while in trance. In his waking condition, Cayce was innocent of any occult inclinations, but his oracular pronunciations have made him a leading figure in the occult revolution.

As with other areas of his "teachings," to which we shall devote some attention in a subsequent chapter, Cayce never developed a unified astrological scheme. However, his disciples have extracted pertinent references from the nearly fifty thousand pages of transcribed readings Cayce gave during his 68 years.

Running against the grain of tradition, Cayce asserted the superiority of free will over the inclinations of the planets. Nevertheless, he clearly stated that the positions of some of the planets directly influence human behavior mainly because of the relationship each of them has in Cayce's teaching to the metempsychotic development of man. Cayce had little use for the traditional significance of aspects, houses, and signs, although he emphasized the importance of cusps. His reason for disavowing the tradition was apparently the disjunction between the tropical and sidereal zodiacs produced by the precession of the equinoxes. Each planet and some stars were for Cayce simply spiritual "planes" which become the school of souls between their incarnations on the "earth plane" of physical existence.

Certain glands of the human body were also identified with the planets in a Caycean system of correspondences unlike any other in astrology or magical lore but certainly reflecting the tendency towards sympathetic associations. Thus Jupiter was related to the pituitary gland, Mercury to the pineal, and so forth in a sort of synthesis of astrological physiology and yoga.

By a strange reversal of karmic polarities, Cayce believed, as had Kepler, that men could affect the celestial environment as well as be affected by it. Sun spots, for instance, were for Cayce equally the cause and effect of communications difficulties on earth—except for the fact that the initial breakdown in human communication is seen to be sin. By creating strife and turmoil on earth, men disrupt the cosmos itself which in turn disturbs human life, thus producing more confusion, uncertainty, and disharmony.

Cayce described the planetary influences on earth-bound human beings in terms of "vibrations," a term found in the traditional vocabulary of spiritualists and now in the hip patois of the counter culture. Such planetary forces are nowhere defined, but Cayce likened them to the effects of any determinate but intangible environment, such as the different "spirits" found among Harvard, Yale, Oxford, and Stanford students.

Thus Cayce's astrological teachings combine cosmic karma and his doctrine of reincarnation to explain the effects of (for example) Neptune's transits. Whatever experiences befell the subject of one of his readings during a spiritual sojourn there before birth are now latent influences responsive to the present position of Neptune as revealed in the subject's horoscope. Such influences operate as psychological stimuli affecting consciousness indirectly. But the vibrations are not merely mental. Cayce once rhapsodized, "For is it not strange that music, color, and vibration are all a part of the planets, just as the planets are a part—and a pattern—of the whole universe?"[5] Not unlike Kepler's "music of the spheres," the mere thought of which often wafted the mystical astronomer to ecstatic flights.

With Cayce, perhaps the most surprising thing is not the eccentric common sense of his astrological observations in comparison to much of the official cant of professional seers, but the fact that he was, in his waking state, as ignorant of astrology as he was of astronomy and medicine. Yet much of his doctrine parallels traditional beliefs and when he departed from accepted explanations, he often offered more coherent interpretations. The rest of his teachings share a remarkably consistent fundament with Cayce's astrology; there are very few contradictions in his entire and enormous body of teachings. Further, his decided emphasis on the role of the planets' positions resembles some surprising new theories being proposed by researchers such as Michel Gauquelin and reflected in new lines of investigation by environmentalists.

[5] Gammon, *Astrology and the Edgar Cayce Readings,* page 25.

Times of the Signs: Astrology vs. Technocracy

Although ridiculed by orthodox scientists since Galileo, with a few exceptions such as Jung, astrology may be on the verge of a scientific reassessment which will produce an understanding of man's relation to his environment equally startling to occultists and ecologists. Man is beginning to be considered a citizen of the entire cosmos once again, sensitive and responsive to all the forces of his environment—terrestial and celestial—the most powerful of which he may totally ignore, as a fish does water.

Let us consider briefly the effects of the sun, moon, planets, and stars now conceded to be operative or under investigation. First, all life on a gross level depends radically on sunlight and solar heat and in particular do green plants, which employ solar energy directly to synthesize carbohydrates. All our food is sunlight and chemical elements. Life itself may well have originated from the impact of solar radiation on complex crystalline compounds; primitive living matter has been produced in laboratories under such conditions. Sunspots are known to produce changes in the composition of human blood corresponding to an eleven-year cycle, a fact first discovered by Dr. Maki Takata of Tokyo in the forties. Heart disease, epidemics, and the suicide rate seem to be linked to the same cycle, and growth patterns revealed in geological strata indicate a similar relationship. Seismic activity within the earth's crust shows another eleven-year cycle, while auroras and radio interference are produced by solar storms which reach their peak every eleven years. Dr. Giorgio Piccardi of Florence and RCA's John Nelson have published findings indicating the effects of solar radiation on chemical reactions and telephone communications. The discovery of animals' built-in "biological clocks" which are responsive to solar and lunar cycles was the result of careful experimentation by Dr. Frank Brown of Northwestern University and Harvard's Dr. Harlan Stetson. In 1938 Dr. Ellsworth Huntington of Yale established a correlation between the month of birth and one's choice of occupation, research originally undertaken by Karl Ernst Krafft in Germany during the thirties and elaborated by Michel and Susan Gauquelin in France within the last decade.

The moon also plays an important role in the gross and subtle events of terrestial existence. The tides have long since been associated with the rotation of our satellite, thousands of years before gravity was given a name. Brown and Caspar have demonstrated as well the lunar rhythm of animal behavior. The human female's menstrual cycle is even named for the moon and corresponds (unlike that of other animals) to the lunar month. Long-held beliefs concerning heightened agitation of mental patients during a full moon, as well as an increase in the crime rate, especially acts of "passion" and arson, are being investigated statistically with some positive results.

The major planets are believed by some to be associated with earthquakes and volcanic eruptions much as is the sun, operating by gravitational attraction. In Australia, Dr. E. G. Bowen has shown that magnetic storms are more frequent when Venus or Mercury are in "inferior conjunction," that is, between the earth and the sun. The responsiveness of planets to magnetic fields is being studied at research institutes throughout the world, suggesting that living tissue may react in decidedly different ways under different gravitational conditions, a fact of considerable importance for the space programs. Solar storms and sunspots, which produce potent "winds" of radiation, are considered to be a function of gravitational interference created by conjunctions of the major planets. During the "magnetic storms" which such events produce on earth, there is, significantly, an increase in the number of mental patients admitted to hospitals. Unfortunately, the nature of gravity and magnetism, like that of electricity, is still a mystery to science. Nevertheless, all life as we know it exists in such electromagnetic and gravitational fields. Nerve impulses are chemico-electrical reactions, and even brain waves seem to be electrical radiations since they are measurable by devices such as electroencephalographs.

Stars, galaxies, and nebulae, plus the mysterious sources of electrical, high-energy radiation called quasars, pulsars, and the eerie black "holes" in space, "collapsars," all have measurable effects on earth. The most potent source of extra-terrestrial gamma radiation comes from the constellation Sagittarius, and ultra-high-energy X-rays emanate most strongly from Scorpius. The hidden depths of nebulae are sources of high-frequency radio waves. Such facts have importance; even the process of aging and the incidence of cancer seem to be related in some way to cosmic radiation.

Less remote environmental conditions have known effects on mankind—background radiation, atmospheric conditions such as temperature, pressure, humidity, the degree and quality of ionization in the air, and so on. It has, for insance, been claimed that a higher death rate experienced during an atmospheric inversion is a consequence of excessive positive ionization. Such an increase was experienced in London on November 4, 1952. Urban man may see more of these "eco-catastrophes" as a direct result of industrial air pollution. Other effects of weather conditions on life have been the subject of intense study by Dr. A. L. Tchijewski of the University of Moscow since 1926 and, in this country, by Dr. William Peterson at the University of Illinois. Dr. Robert Becker of the Veterans' Administration Hospital in Syracuse has been investigating similar conditions in relation to variations in the body's electromagnetic field.

All this, of course, is very remote indeed from the royal art. But there is considerable room for speculation. It may not seem likely that the gravitational force of the sun, moon, or larger planets can have a direct effect on human destiny, if for no other reason than men are rather minuscule organisms in proportion to the planets and stars—an historical objection to astrology. We know, for instance, that a mere hundred miles above the earth the force of gravity on an orbiting astronaut is equalized so that every body in the universe is exercising approximately the same attraction, which enables orbiting to occur in the first place. As Newton realized, the force of gravity bears an inverse relationship to the distance between two bodies, but is directly proportional to the masses of the interacting bodies. Hence, even the great mass of the sun can exercise only a relatively minor influence on a very small body such as a human being. Similarly, the electromagnetic influence of Jupiter is relatively minor in terms of its effect on any individual person or even on all human beings. Together, all the planets, stars, and galaxies will have much less influence on us than will our own planet. On the other hand, a planet such as Mars or Venus, or even the moon, must have a great effect gravitationally on the *whole* earth because of the mass of the bodies despite the great distances separating them. Consequently, a force-field exists between all the planets of the solar system and in the central star. And we tiny beings live in that field, experiencing similar but lesser influences than plants, for example, "feel" in an artificially created magnetic field, which inclines them to develop in determinable fashion.

Astrologically, if a powerful force-field exists between the moon, sun, and earth with respect to the other planets, which would be much stronger than a field existing with respect to an individual person on earth, there will nevertheless be some effect on earth-bound creatures, however indirect. Further, since these celestial bodies are always moving with regard to the earth, there is a synergic effect created by the interacting patterns and a consequent differentiation in the character of the field at any given time. Such variations are analogous to the differences in agricultural conditions that produce dissimilar qualities of crops—for instance, grapes and their wines. Carl Jung is reputed to have stated that "We are born at a given moment, in a given place and, like vintage years of wine, we have the qualities of the year and of the season in which we are born. Astrology does not lay claim to anything more."[5]

A generation of people born when the planets were in certain conjunctions may well have similar, specifiable characteristics. Scientifically speaking, it is questionable why the moment of birth should be more important than the moment of conception (another perennial objection), although at birth a child exists for the first time outside the protecting environment of his mother's womb and is directly exposed to the conditions of radiation, climate, and so forth. One possible explanation for the emphasis on the new sensitivities of the just-born is that exposure to the "world" begins immediately to affect the nervous system and the brain, which are delicately tuned electrical transceivers, emitting signals of a specific pattern and frequency.

Given all this, it seems possible that cosmic conditions can affect people physiologically and psychologically in term of the interacting relationships of the sun, moon, and planets. A child born during a magnetic storm would likely bear in his make-up the effects of such disturbance. By implication, there may well be a basis for astrological claims if for no other purpose than as a psychological short-hand by which we can describe character traits based on planetary configurations. At any rate, based on thousands of years of observation, there does seem to be an un-canny correspondence between traditional astrological interpre-tations of character based on the sun-sign as modified by the positions of the moon and planets.

As we learn more about the human personality in its engage-ment with the total environment, with all the psychological and physiological mechanisms that operate whether we know it or not, it may well prove beneficial to consider the age-old royal art as well as other phenomena relegated to the dusty nooks of the

[5] Quoted in Pagan and Leo, *The Coffee Table Book of Astrology,* page 3.

occult. They may one day explain a great deal about human life and behavior that remain at present inexplicable or unknown.

Uranus and the Age of Aquarius

Considered from a mythological point of view (that is,. symbolically), astrological expectations focus many hopes and fears expressed in other ways concerning the near and also distant future. The Age of Pisces, the Christian era, is yielding to that of Aquarius, the era of the Holy Spirit according to Jung—an airy time of peace, understanding, and love ruled over by the strange planet Uranus, who represents sudden changes, revolution, invention, and scientific discovery. From a spiritual viewpoint, the coming age will be one of transformations and new vision. Both astrology and its chief opponents, organized religion and science, will probably appear in different guise to the new generations of the third millennium. But even today, astrology has something of value to contribute to mankind, and religion and science may benefit.

Astrology affirms the profound ecological unity of all creation. We can no longer conceive of man as a being apart from the rest of the universe—physically, mentally, or spiritually. The ecological backlash we are beginning to dread is, perhaps, the greatest example of karmic retribution conceivable this side of Armageddon: the wasted earth will have its say. Unlike more respectable disciplines, astrology has always seen man as a child of the cosmos, free but influenced in body and spirit by the conditions of the environment. It is therefore not surprising that the royal art has found a new allegiance among the ecologically oriented young; it presents a thoroughly human approach to the domestic universe.

Another beneficial influence of astrology may be its emphasis on personal integration—a synthesis of personal powers and inclinations that enables us to adjust well to both the social and

93

physical environments. Unfortunately, most popular exposure to astrology is not that of Dane Rudhyar's folk-psychology, but the journalistic pabulum of the daily horoscope columns which, while not in themselves harmful as advice, can too easily nourish the cancer of superstition. The chief danger of popular astrological enthusiasm is that it is habit-forming and can easily begin to influence our thinking and acting. By dint of the "halo effect," one unlikely coincidence can win a convert to such cheap counselling despite the majority of wholly inaccurate predictions. No matter how sophisticated we are, no matter how innocuous the advice given, relying on prefabricated counsel for the conduct of our lives will have its baneful influence on us, creating at worst a real psychological dependence. There are people we all know or have heard about who cannot begin their day's work without consulting the daily oracle. Surrendering our birthright of freedom and responsibility for the mess of pottage in the newspaper columns is dehumanizing—both un-astrological in the traditional view and thoroughly anti-Christian. A great deal of house-cleaning will be needed before astrology can make its contribution in the area of advice.

A third, perhaps less positive area of contribution is the hint we have detected from the astrological mania that religion and science are not at present satisfying the expectations of the young. In a world of uncertainty, indeterminacy, and skepticism, astrology's ancient, somewhat immutable doctrine is a comforting source of theoretical and practical information. In this it shares the attractiveness of other elements of the occult revolution apart from any religious or scientific basis. Its very persecution by the Church and academy stand astrology in a favorable position for the young critics of the technocratic way of life.

Lastly, astrology is attractive because it is fun as well as fascinating. It provides a basis for conversation and meditation—knowing that an acquaintance was born under Gemini or Aries reassures us, also, that we are not so alien as we may have been led to believe.

As a counter-cultural phenomenon, astrology provides an alternative mode of responding to the demands of the space age, a humanistic rather than technological affirmation of man's position of nobility in the midst of a vast cosmos. He does not have to be an astronaut to be a citizen of the universe, a "cosmopolitan lover" as Sam Keen prefers it. The planets and stars are nonetheless once again manageable.

The rise of astrological popularity is also an index to the loss of confidence that many have expressed in the organized churches. In his *Dictionary of Astrology*, Dal Lee writes: "Since the Aquarian conjunction of February 1962, the world of organized religion seems to have fallen apart. The clergy have lost control of the masses; the bishops have lost control of the clergy; and it seems the Supreme Intelligence has lost control of the bishops."[6]

Many of the young in particular "no longer trust the Churches," and thus they have turned to astrology as they turned to yoga, Zen, drugs, and witchcraft—not so much knowing what they would find in it, but willing to take the gamble. Of such is the Age of Aquarius.

[6] New York, 1968, page 20.

95

6.

Witchcraft—The Old Religion as a New Cult

NOT only England, but all of Europe from the Renaissance to the Middle Ages, witnessed the savage torture and hecatombs of eccentric old women, envied young girls, and other hated members of a town or village variously known as witches—whether men or women, or even children, the mad and deluded, Jews and vagabonds. Most were innocent victims, though there were a few practitioners of magical arts who indeed dabbled in dark doings. This hateful frenzy, which was recognized for its dramatic potential only with Arthur Miller's *The Crucible,* succeeded in convulsing much of continental Europe, England, Scotland, and New England for almost three centuries and cost the lives of perhaps 300,000 victims, not to mention the untold suffering of hundreds of thousands more who were imprisoned, pilloried, tortured, and fined before they were released. And now, two hundred years later, witchcraft has suddenly reappeared in Chicago, New York, and London—on the streets, on television (*Bewitched*), and in comic strips (*Broomhilda* and even *Dondi*), as well as in films, magazines, newspapers, and other media of society.

Most of us share a notion of witchery derived from the medieval caricature and sanctioned by Walt Disney's *Snow White and the Seven Dwarfs*—a wizened old hag, her warty nose nearly meeting her chin, dressed in black rags, mean and slightly batty, cacklingly preparing poisons and other sinister goodies. But like the weird sisters of *Macbeth,* the Halloween witch with pointed hat and broomstick, accompanied by her cat (a role wonderfully incarnated by Margaret Hamilton in *The Wizard of Oz*, but one she never escaped) bears remote resemblance indeed to the chic, mini-skirted secretaries that adorn the hundreds of covens in the United States and Europe.

Contemporary witches also insist that their "craft" is in reality the present-day continuation of "the old religion": primitive beliefs and rites that antedate Christianity and all other organized religions. And they are young; despite the fact that the best-known witches such as Sybil Leek are in their middle years, most witch covens consist of women (and men!) in their twenties and early thirties. But occasionally, I have met a teenage witch, and even children have been initiated into covens it would seem.

These young "dissenters" deny any connection with satanism as it is traditionally known, an element of occultism they fear and despise. Their brand of witchcraft employs (if such terminology is used at all) "white" magic—the natural powers latent in the human body and spirit. Gods and spirits may be summoned by a coven, but this is a far cry from the conjurations of necromancers and second-rate wizards of old, intent on selling their souls to Satan for money, youth, or (less likely) wisdom. Conversely, there are many apparently "satanic" cults which are not witch covens and do not practice any kind of magic, just as there are truly satanic churches that advertise magical rites, such as Anton LaVey's Church of Satan in San Francisco. "Black" magic likewise exists, at least by intent, and sometimes a coven will fall under the power of a "black" magician, but such groups are reported to be the arch-enemies of the "white" witch covens. The dictionary description covers both possibilities, defining a witch as "one who practices the black art of magic; one regarded as possessing supernatural or magic power by compact with an evil spirit, especially with the devil; a sorcerer or sorceress."

Unfortunately, so much contradictory material about witchcraft is available, as well as various superficial accounts which are even more bewildering, that it is extremely difficult to produce a coherent account of either ancient or modern witches. Much of the historical testimony of the witches themselves, even that which was freely volunteered and not extracted by ınhuman tortures (the more likely alternative), is suspect today as it was for a few reasonable men in the heyday of the Inquisition. What is not in question is that thousands of Americans, Europeans, Asians, Latin Americans, and Africans still profess to be witches and engage in that craft, although some of the cultural variations might startle a Manhattan sybarite.

According to recent accounts, there are over six thousand witches in England (a country historically favored by them), and upwards of five thousand in New York City, with equivalent numbers bewitching in San Francisco, Los Angeles, Chicago, Detroit, and other major cities, as well as in towns and villages. Reports of typical coven activities indicate that modern witches primarily engage in somewhat exotic rituals, no doubt a welcome relief from the drab world of office and apartment, rather than the more pedestrian occupations of African, Haitian, or Jamaican witches—curing blisters, finding lost valuables, charming animals, and (occasionally) killing enemies. But both kinds of witchcraft exist in the world today, often surprisingly proximate.

Like other manifestations of the occult revolution, modern witchcraft signals vast changes in social and religious life and is important as a barometer rather than a menace to Church or state. The tortuous history of witchcraft, despite its complexities, will either substantiate or repudiate that contention. Whatever the outcome of the comparison, witchcraft has again become something to reckon with.

Ancient Witchcraft: Daughters of Darkness

From anthropological data, archeological records, and the literature of classical antiquity, it is demonstrably certain that in addition to the magicians and priests characteristic of all peoples, there were official and unofficial prophets, soothsayers, and a distinct class of uncivil servants who dispensed cures, mended (or broke) hearts, recovered lost and stolen property, summoned the dead, and told the future more or less by the aid of a tutelar spirit or "familiar." In English-speaking countries, such persons, of both genders, inherited the Anglo-Saxon title *wicce* (masculine, *wicca*). Latin authors had a variety of names for those practitioners of the arts whom we lump together under the single rubric of witchcraft: a female witch might be known as an *incantatrix, lamia, maga, malefica, saga, sortilega* (which later became "sorceress"), *strix* (a vampire) and the poison-peddler or *venefica*.

Since contemporary witches place so much importance on the connection between the words "witch" and "wise," it might be appropriate to note that the etymology involved is less authentic than the anthropology; the two words have nothing in common. *Wicce* simply means "witch," deriving through the Old English *"wiccian"* from the Germanic *"Wikken,"* and here the trail disappears. "Wise" was rendered by *"wis"* or *"wys,"* as in *"wizard"* (wys-ard), whose origin is from the same Indo-European word as the Latin *"videre"* and the Greek *"oida"*: the Sanskrit *"veda,"* meaning "to see." A wizard, incidentally, was a man whose relation to wisdom was like a drunkard's to drink. More humorous yet, a "warlock" was a deceiver, a covenant-breaker; *"waer"* being a pact or covenant, and *"loga"* meant "liar" or "breaker." Anglo-Saxon writers called their *wiccas* "warlocks" out of sheer contempt, and no self-respecting wizard would have countenanced the title. However, the patent nonsense of the witches' attempts at respectability should not blind us to the significance of the attempt. As with the medieval conception of the witches' role, the ancient words are twisted to present us with the "fact" that witches are not what we think they are. And that is true.

In olden days, witches were not believed to have derived their power from evil spirits nor probably even from a familiar. Thus Circe in Homer's *Odyssey* is merely a sorceress (a word which stems from the Latin "*sors*," meaning "lots," and referring to destiny)—a beautiful, regal, and somewhat unpleasant woman who amuses herself by changing men into beasts. Agamede and the old necromancer Tiresias in the *Iliad* are also witches, as is the mysterious Oenothea of Apuleius's *The Golden Ass,* whose story is beautifully portrayed in Fellini's film *Satyricon.* Most of these ancient witches were associated with animals, and belief in their ability to transform themselves or others into beasts is associated with the legends of werewolves and changelings. And although most witches were not exactly evil, their morality was certainly as variable as their appearance, and all were awesome and feared.

Some of the oldest writings in the world deal with witchcraft in its most primitive form. One of the Assyrian magic tablets laments that "the sorcerer has bewitched me with the spell . . . He who enchants images has charmed away my life by magic." The Hebrew scriptures placed the ban on sorcery early in the history of the Chosen People: "Thou shalt not suffer a witch to live" would be remembered for centuries as the justification for killing those convicted of witchcraft, for these were the words of God to Moses (Ex. 22, 18). The actual meaning of the word ("*kashaph*") in Hebrew is disputed.

In the first book of Samuel, chapter 28, we read of Saul's visit to the "witch" ("*ba' alath ob*") of Endor, a necromancer who raised up the shade of Samuel for Saul, but the ghost thereupon predicted the king's impending ruin as a punishment for abandoning the ways of the Lord. King Manasseh, following in the steps of Solomon (who according to tradition was a mighty sorcerer), sacrificed his own children to Moloch in the Valley of Hinnom (the later Gehenna), practiced astrological divination, consulted magicians, and summoned the dead (2 Kings 21, 6; cf. 2 Chr. 33, 6). Although Manasseh was perhaps engaging in a bit of practical ecumenism in the midst of the multiplex "old religions" of the ancient Near East, to the prophets and even more to the demon-obsessed Jacobites of seventeenth-century England, he was in league with Satan himself, a very devil in human form.

Isaiah was paramount among the prophets of Israel for his distaste for all the occult arts. A savage satirist, he called to the Hebrews: "Stand now with thine enchantments, and with the multitude of thy sorceries, wherein thou hast labored from thy youth; if so be thou shalt be able to profit, if so be thou mayest prevail. Thou art wearied in the multitude of thy counsels. Let now the astrologers, the stargazers, the monthly prognosticators stand up and save thee from these things that shall come upon thee" (47, 12–13).

Outside the Hebrew tradition, Euripides and Aristophanes among the Greeks and the Roman naturalist Pliny the Elder and the poets Lucan, Virgil, Ovid, and Horace agree that the origin of witchcraft lay in Thessaly, north of Greece. They also concur in identifying Medea, Circe's niece, as another powerful enchantress. Demosthenes had spoken of Theodoris of Lemnos, and Tacitus writes of the Druid priestess Vellada of Gaul in similar fashion. The fourth century of the Christian era produced Mary the Jewess, whose name is associated with the alchemists' double-boiler, the *bain-marie,* which she may have invented. In the same century, a Frankish queen named Fredegonde was supposedly possessed of the evil eye and practiced witchcraft, the rumor of which at least would serve to enhance her power. Shortly thereafter, as Christianity conquered the lands of the *pagani,* witchcraft began to take on an ever more sinister aspect: the gods of the old religions were associated (as had been the gods of the Greeks and Romans) with demons, to whose blame could be laid any obstacles to evangelization.

In his *Praeparatio Evangelica,* Eusebius (who died in 309) attributes the origin of magic and, *a fortiori,* witchcraft to evil

101

angels, reflecting Talmudic legends about Adam's dalliance with the vampire Lilith, the story of the Watchers, and other myths. Lilith, who became a night-monster and bane of children's stories, even wandered into the pages of Scripture itself (Is. 34, 4, and Prov. 30, 15), as other monsters, demons, and sorcerers also found their places in the Bible up to and pre-eminently in the Book of Revelation. Eastern Christianity was particularly, though by no means exclusively, preoccupied with demons, especially the lustful imps whose delight was in tempting the Desert Fathers. Given such a tendency towards belief in the demonic, it should not surprise us that early writers, such as the apologists, blended elements of classical demonology with the lore of witches and magicians and the whole pagan pantheon. Augustine, for instance, opposed all forms of magical art as demonic, an association that became the patrimony of the West as Islam eclipsed Eastern theological speculation.

The transition from enmity between Church leaders and the witches to all-out persecution did not occur without some intervening contributions from the state. In the ninth century, Charlemagne sentenced to death any apprehended "agents of the devil who arouse tempests." Similar legislation was enacted under Aelfred, Edward I, Ethelstan, and Edgar in England. Even so, at that time an obscure Council of Ancrya seems to have decreed that women who believed and professed that they flew through the air to revels presided over by Diana, the moon goddess, were merely deluded. Priests were therefore instructed to preach against such nonsense, which itself was a wicked notion sent by the Evil One. From the prestige later accorded this decree, which became known as the *Canon Episcopi,* we can conclude that at this time the Church refused official credence to tales of night-flying witches and Sabbaths, while nonetheless reiterating injunctions against sorcery, divination, and other black arts. What changed the official position of the Chuch from incredulity to persecution was nothing less than a religious revolution.

A Medieval Synthesis: From Armageddon to Salem

As the year 1000 approached, rumors spread through Europe that the world would end at that time or that Satan would then inaugurate the reign of the Anti-Christ, alluded to in Revelation. Eschatological expectation ran ever higher as the tenth century waned, and then, in the first fateful year of the second millennium, no less a portent than a great comet appeared in the Western sky. Earthquakes and volcanic eruptions devastated Italy, while famine and pestilence ravaged the rest of Europe. Terror gripped whole nations as the "End" approached. But the year passed, and yet another came and went. The Day of Judgment had been postponed, but the awful events of that year and the eschatological mania that preceded and fed on them would not be forgotten.

A tide of religious fervor quickly engulfed Western Europe. In the space of a single lifetime, the Crusades were summoned to free the Holy Land, the mysterious Cistercian Abbot Joachim of Flora predicted the coming of a new world age, the mendicant orders appeared and began to restore the shaky soul of Christendom, and the great Gothic cathedrals began to rise heavenward, as if the grateful world were expressing its thanks in stone. Commerce flourished, cities grew and prospered, national states began to emerge from the chaos of the Dark Ages, the universities were founded. Europe had discovered sinew and exuberant daring in its brush with the Destroying Angel and displayed its coming of age in feats of mind and will.

In many respects, however, the brilliant new face of civilization merely covered over the repressed savagery of barbarian warlords and brutalized serfs. Superstition, fear, and ignorance still lurked deep in men's minds. The magnificent Crusades became the occasion for pillage, rapine, and slaughter, the schismatic Greeks and "infidel" Jews falling victim to fire and sword no less than Saracens and Turks. Anti-Semitism spread cancerously in the shadows of cathedrals and monasteries. And finally, repelled in the East, the Christian monarchs launched yet another Crusade in the West against the enemies of Christ: the Cathars and Albigensians who worshipped, it was said, a god of evil co-equal to the Christian God. The Cathari were accused of riding on broomsticks or rods smeared with a magic oil to attend their heathen assemblies, and of murdering children and making potions from their bodies. The devil was believed to appear in the form of a cat at their festivals and was given homage by being kissed under his tail.

In 1215 Pope Innocent III created the Inquisition, a Church tribunal before which accused heretics were brought for examination. A more insidious instrument of destruction could scarcely have been devised. Determined to eradicate heresy, Judaism, and Mohammedan influence, the Inquisitors soon discovered an even more dangerous threat to the Church, and the magician, diviner, and witch were examined along with other suspected enemies of the faith. The first witch trials date from about 1245 in the region of Toulouse. There a woman was burned alive in 1275, having been accused of witchcraft and sexual liaison with the devil. At this early date, the penalty for witchcraft itself was rarely capital, as had been the case in the Dark Ages, and burning was generally reserved for heretics, traitors, and poisoners. In 1324, for instance, the maid of Dame Agnes Kyteler (or Kettle) was burned alive in Ireland for aiding her mistress, a sorceress, to kill four husbands by poison and enchantments. Lady Agnes herself escaped to England. (Very few instances of witchcraft persecution occurred in Ireland; though one of them involved a sadly ironic case of the death of a black slave whose master confused necromancy with "negromancy.")

Descriptions of witches' Sabbaths and night rides on broomsticks nowhere appear at this early date, nor will they for another century, owing to the authority of the *Canon Episcopi*. Similarly, no detailed account of witchcraft would appear for over a hundred years. But the groundwork for a systematic purge was being inadvertently laid.

In 1346 a terrible pestilence swept over Europe, leaving in its aftermath the bodies of perhaps a third of the population of the Continent and the British Isles. Soon, the smouldering coals of apocalyptic fears were fanned to fever heat by packs of obsessed preachers and hordes of penitents wandering the countrysides, flagellating themselves, fasting, and calling on the spectators to join them. In many places, it was believed that, first, Jews and then witches had conspired with Satan to bring about the Black Death, and many innocent victims fell into the hands of lynch mobs and half-legal executioners. So entrenched had the belief in witchcraft become in Europe in this frantic search for a sacrificial scapegoat, that within a century even the *Canon Episcopi* was overturned, the reason being that the witches of the early fifteenth century were a *new* sect, and the ancient restriction no longer applied. Diabolical allegiance, power to sicken or kill, hatred of the Church, and hostility towards society were the criminal credentials of the witches. Similar accusations, such as those of a diabolical pact, the "kiss of shame," sacrilege, and sexual perversion were used by Philip IV of France to destroy the Knights Templar, whose considerable estates and wealth were confiscated by the crown. Burning was the penalty upon conviction, whether for Templar or common witch, and thus it would remain until the end of the seventeenth century except for England, where burning was reserved for traitors and heretics.

Portrait of a Witch

The anxieties of life in the middle fourteenth century provided ample scope for the enlargement of witchcraft fantasies during the search for the scapegoats by whose sacrifice some surcease might come. It is one of the greatest and most ironic tragedies of

Western civilization that the portrait of the witch was limned by the Inquisitors out of their own fears, lusts, and superstitions —men who, in their repressed savagery, forced hundreds of thousands of innocent people to sign prepared confessions by the threat and use of the most inhuman tortures. Thus, to the minds of the investigators, that which they sought to prove was adequately demonstrated, and men, women, and children were consigned to the stake, hanged, or beheaded by the thousands.

From their confessions, plus the accounts of investigations and trials published in handbooks such as the *Malleus Malificarum* ("Hammer of Witches") of 1484 and the much later *Compendium Malificarum,* printed in 1604, a general impression of the "witch" and her craft in Renaissance and seventeenth-century Europe emerges, a portrait which, if it does not represent a real phenomenon, at least describes the popular belief. A witch was generally a woman, young or old (although there were both male and child witches), who in return for her allegiance to Satan or some lesser demon was given power over people, crops, animals, storms, accidents, pestilence, and fire. The liturgical worship of Satan, later enlarged into a parody of the Catholic Mass, first in belief, then in reality to a very limited degree, stood witchcraft in direct opposition to the Church and its sacraments in the minds of the clergy. (Both Catholic and Reformer were relentless in their hatred of witches; Luther remarked in his *Table Talk,* "I would have no pity on these witches; I would burn them all.") The Black Mass as an integral characteristic of witchcraft is, however, a late addition, appearing in southern France late in the fifteenth century and only gradually spreading north, where by the time the belief reached Commonwealth England, it was then a counter-Calvinist prayer-meeting.

Among the most ancient singular attributes of a witch are her ability to enchant by spells, incantations, charms, or even a simple glance—the feared "evil eye" or *fascinatio; transvection* —the power of nocturnal flight, usually requiring a broom or hayfork and a preliminary rub-down with a magic salve; and *metamorphosis*—the ability to change into animal form, a quality which became confused with the presence of a "familiar" spirit which was often in animal form, such as a black cat or dog, a mouse or toad or various kinds of birds, especially ravens. This feature both lent and borrowed from the legends of were-animals.

As a mark of his favor or as a sign of a witch's commitment to Satan, she was supposed to possess a "devil's mark," some small sign on her flesh, usually insensitive to pain and well-hidden. Searching for these on the bodies of the accused gave the self-righteous interrogators great opportunity to peer at human nakedness and satisfy truly sadistic impulses: accused witches were often probed with "prickers"—cruel implements resembling an ice-pick which, it was claimed, would pierce the witch's mark without pain. (Needless to say, by the time the accusers located a "mark," the wretched victim had experienced sufficient pain that she likely had lost sensibility.) Some of these instruments, to be on the "safe" side, had retractable points which slipped into a hollow handle equipped with a spring-mechanism, creating the appearance of entering the body "painlessly." Many of these "prickers" can be seen in museums. Matthew Hopkins, England's notorious witch-hunter, who was responsible for thousands of innocent people being hanged, possessed at least one of these devilish tools, by the generous use of which he made himself the scourge of Essex in the seventeenth century.

Another irrefutable sign of witchhood was the "witch's teat," a supernumerary nipple on a woman's body (men sometimes have them as well) by which the suspect was supposed to be able to suckle her familiar with either milk or blood. Searching for these uncommon but nonetheless existent physiological abnormalities became another favorite pursuit of the witch hunters Needless to say they sometimes succeeded, for even today perhaps 10 per cent of a given population will bear that or a similar anomaly.

On a collective level, the revelry of witches at their "Sabbaths" became a favorite theme of the trials, and such events were described by the persecutors with lurid detail, along with tales of devil-worship, the Black Mass, ritual cannibalism, wild dancing, and orgiastic debauches—anything lewd or sacrilegious, and preferably both. By the strange processes of human suggestibility, many witches, whether real or supposed, began to accept such fabrications as true incidents and sometimes elaborated on the accounts created by the Inquisitors. It remains a fact, however, that the original outlines of such phenomena were sketched not by the accused but by their accusers.

Witches' revels and Cathar "synagogues" early became merged in the creative minds of the Inquisitors, and by the kind of logic involved in such processes, soon the devil was a guest of honor at the "Sabbaths," being worshipped by the witches, copulating with them, and presiding over the general orgy which concluded the ritual assembly. Often he appeared in the form of a cat or dog, but by 1458, his chosen incarnation seems to have been the form of a goat. In that year, for example, an old man freely confessed that at a Sabbath, his mother had long before dedicated him, his sister, and his baby brother to the devil, who was seen as a goat and whose touch bestowed an indelible mark on them all. The reporter who copied the confession was Nicholas Jacquier, who declared in that year (1458) that witchcraft was a new heresy and therefore beyond the aegis of the *Canon Episcopi*.

Witchcraft and devil-worship were inextricably associated in the minds of the Inquisitors and subsequently their victims'— a "marriage of convenience" not hindered by the crusade against the hated Luciferans (1227), who had, it seems, actually worshipped Satan. That the devil preferred the form of a goat is significant from an anthropological viewpoint with respect to the history of religions. Although there is no conclusive evidence that the ancient worship of Pan or the Druids' Cernurnos, both of whom were horned divinities, was thus identified as demonic by Christians, there can be little doubt that the "Goat of Mendes" was related to pagan ritual. In the Dark Ages, Caesarius of Arles, Theodore of Canterbury, and the Fathers of the Council of Auxerre testified that many people masqueraded in animal skins for certain festivals and dances. Among the antics of these maskers, which survived well into the medieval period, was the wearing of a horned head-piece. Whatever the original significance of donning the "horned helmet," Theodore of Canterbury had no doubt about its contemporary meaning: "This is devilish," he fumed. Such practices were eventually severely prohibited. It is to this ancient, "devilish" custom that modern witches trace their lineage, happy to span the intervening years of diabolical association and persecutions.

The use of the word *"Sabbath"* has been variously accounted for, but common opinion suggests that it betrays not only anti-Cathar sentiment, but also anti-Semitic prejudice, a notion supported by the association of medieval Jewish mysticism (cabalism) with magic, as well as the use of the word *"synagogue"* for the Cathar assemblies. Both Jews and Cathars were thought to be in league with wizards and witches, wreaking doom on hapless Christians. That witches had Sabbath assemblies was never seriously doubted after 1458 until the end of the seventeenth century. As many as six or seven thousand witches were believed to gather for the great Sabbaths, most of which corresponded the pagan holidays and their Christian counterparts. There were eight in all: the summer and winter solstices, the spring and autumnal equinoxes, and four dates in between— May eve or Walpurgisnacht, on April 30; Lammas on August 1; Hallowmas on November 1; and Candelmas, near February 1. Sabbaths were supposedly held at night, which meant that, like Walpurgisnacht, the eve of St. Walpurga's Day, the night previous to the Christian or pagan feast was celebrated, giving us Hallowe'en, Lammaseve, and the even of the feast of St. John on the vernal equinox, June 24. Such dates reflect the Celtic calendar, as contemporary witches recall, for Beltane (May 1) and Samhain (November 1) marked the beginning of summer and winter, thus dividing the year. The Christian Church, following a policy of competitive accommodation, had, in the eighth century, moved its feast of All Hallows or Hallowmas from the original date (May 13), which had been a Roman feast of the vampire Lemures, to November 1. The idea of a Sabbath assembly, probably indicating a Saturday revel, fitted the pattern of pre-holiday sacrilege by anticipating the Christians' First Day or Sunday. Strangely, Sabbaths were actually held to be celebrated at any time during the week, and today, only the eight great festivals are known by that name, monthly get-togethers being more frequently called Esbats, probably from the French "*s'esbettre*" ("to frolic," "to dance"), a word which Margaret Murray—erroneously—considered the origin of *Sabbath*.

The local group of witches was called a *coven,* meaning a gathering or meeting, as in "covenant." The number of members in a coven was supposedly thirteen, perhaps a parody of the number of Apostles and Jesus, including Judas. Covens were alleged to engage in ritual magic, minor orgies, and general trouble-making. Despite the assertions of Montague Summers and Dr. Murray, actual thirteen-member covens do not appear to have existed before the late nineteenth century. When witches did gather for their dire doings (and sometimes this actually happened), the number varied from two or three to perhaps a dozen, but only eighteen cases out of tens of thousands reported by the Inquisitors produced thirteen-member covens, and whether these were actual groups is doubtful. What is not in question is the fact that there *were* people who considered themselves to be witches (as there are today and in plenty) and that they *did* meet on occasion to conspire some mischief or revel. These people were neither victims of torture who would confess to anything for respite, nor were they driven to confess for the sake of notoriety—although there were plenty of cases of both.

The "real" witches, unlike these others, and always a minimal percentage of those accused, often went to their deaths at the stake or gallows professing their devotion to Satan and their hatred for God, Christ, the Church, and their fellow men. That there was never a large number of such miserable creatures was recognized even during the infamous Spanish Inquisition, when more temperate clerics such as Martin del Rio and Salazar Frias refused to accept even voluntary confessions as conclusive proof of guilt. Many people who had been unjustly accused of witchcraft were defended and released through these Inquisitors, often in defiance of popular feeling.

Unlike Spain (and Ireland, where the people had devil enough in the British), most northern European nations, both Catholic and Protestant, mercilessly hunted witches and sorcerers, against whom the slimmest accusations were damning evidence. Authorities believe that in Germany over one hundred thousand persons were executed for witchcraft, mainly during the sixteenth century. In England and her colonies, perhaps ten or twenty thousand were hanged (only fifty or so were hanged in New England), but Scotland burned thousands more. France, Italy, Switzerland, and the Slavic nations had their hecatombs, which were repeated in Scandinavia and the Low Countries. Estimates of the total number who perished vary from 200,000 to 300,000 over a period from 1458 to about 1750.

Not until the Enlightment did the witch mania subside, though witches were still being lynched well into this century. Martin Ebon in *Witchcraft Today* relates that such an incident occurred in Mexico in 1968. But as early as 1584, a century after the bull *Summis Desiderantes* of Innocent VIII, which had unleashed the pent-up fury of Europe against the witches, a level-headed and keen-witted Englishman named Reginald Scot penned a satirical broadside against the folly of the witchcraft mania. His *Discoverie of Witchcraft* so angered King James I —himself a frequent target of Scottish witches, and thus (perhaps understandably) a vehement witch-hater—that the monarch ordered all copies of the book consigned to the flames. In another nation or at another time, Scot might have accompanied them, for as the French politician and witch-hunter Jean Bodin observed, one who defended an accused witch or opposed the persecution, or even professed disbelief in witchcraft entirely, was likely to be a witch.

Scot, thoroughly vilified in James's *Demonologie* (1597) and no better favored by preachers and common folk, nevertheless gained the ear of many intelligent and humane men of letters, and within a generation skeptics such as William Harvey were disproving the most basic tenets of the whole fiasco. But the last official execution of an English witch took place in 1684—a century after Scot wrote. The death penalty was repealed under George II in 1736. Holland had stopped killing witches as early as 1610. The American colonists had called a halt to the frenzy in 1692. Scotland burned its last witch in 1727, France in 1745. In 1775 Germany sent the last witch to the headsman. (The Inquisition, which had been under effective state control since 1480, sadly did not end the use of torture to extract confessions from heretics until 1816.)

With the irony of belated realization, as the demonic investigations that had possessed Europe for three hundred years diminished, so did the "evidence" of witchcraft. Within a generation or two, the only witches worth mention were rural herbalists, animal charmers, and the "white" witches—"good women" and "cunning men" who had been carrying on their traditions since the close of the Dark Ages. A few survive to this day in Europe and in the American Southwest, South, and in the mountain regions such as Appalachia. But any real connection between these people, the hunted witches of the late medieval period, and today's urban secretaries in anything except nomenclature is purely coincidental.

Of course, the decline of persecution is not the only reason for the demise of the public witchcraft mania. Both events were also the result of manifold changes that began with the Renaissance to shake Europe out of its post-medieval lassitude. The telescope was revealing new worlds beyond man's sight while the microscope began to probe new and undreamed-of microcosms of life. Medicine was emerging from the dark world of superstition and barbers' shops; the steam engine would soon revolutionize industry. Chemists were adding new elements to the ancient tables of alchemy. Freedom was in the very air— freedom to inquire as well as political views of libertarianism. Within a century, the map of the world would be transformed, Napoleon would sit on an imperial throne, locomotives would run along iron roadbeds, and men would fly in balloons.

Mod Witchcraft

Contemporary witches are as unlike the Renaissance conception as that was different from the classical notion—excepting the *brujos* and *curanderos,* witch doctors and their ilk who carry on the ancient work in the less urbanized regions of the earth. Even today's sophisticated witches favor the conceit that they are perpetuating an ancient religion rather than carrying on the real tradition of folk medicine, primitive psychotherapy, and ghost chasing. The truth about witchcraft, contrary to the beliefs of its adherents and the opinions of Murray, Summers, and the more contemporary Hans Holzer, is that there is virtually no connection between any of these varieties of magical experience. The significant relation (other than conscious imitation) is the *mental* association—the belief itself, which is of importance to an understanding of the occult revolution.

The daily press carries enough interviews and articles dealing with witchcraft today to constitute something of a survey. Few if any young witches have ever denied that witchcraft is fundamentally a religious movement (unlike, for instance, the protestations of Masons and Rosicrucians). Rather they usually maintain that it is the "old religion" itself, mankind's archetypal cult. Most witches seem to prefer that designation rather than the even less valid "craft of the wise." Whether or not witch covens would be admitted to the National Council of Churches, and regardless of the truth of claims about continuity with paleolithic worship, contemporary witchcraft is foremost of anything a religion. To be more precise, it is a counter religion or, if you prefer, the religion of a counter culture.

"Religion in the traditional sense no longer provides the spiritual guidance and sustenance in times of trouble it used to when the Church was really potent," Hans Holzer explains.[1] Therefore witchcraft provides "to those seeking practical and effective help . . . a reason to get out. And they leave their church and go in search of something else to fill their spiritual void." Most converts to witchery, Holzer discovered, are ex-Catholics disillusioned by the Church's "shallowness." Holzer nevertheless claims that such Catholics and other Christians are really looking for a more liberal form of religion which they find in witchcraft. He concludes that not many members of more liberal churches are converted: "the liberal Christian churches are close enough to the ideals of The Craft not to warrant it."[2] It seems far more likely, however, that conversion to occultism represents a conservative reaction rather than a liberal one—a question to which we shall return in detail later on.

The "religion" which the convert to witchcraft discovers must seem like a meld of small-group encounter sessions and the rituals of a secret society, which is about what it amounts to. Membership in a coven is restricted to thirteen, ideally—an interesting case of Dr. Murray's "anthropological" horse coming far behind the historical cart—including the priest and/or priestess. No trace of night-flights exists in modern witchcraft, nor

[1] *The Truth About Witchcraft,* New York, 1971, page 29.
[2] *Ibid.,* page 30.

do the evil-eye, familiars, metamorphosis, or satanism (for the most part), and although it pretends to be a bona fide pagan religion it is not anti-Christian in any political sense. Most witches are simply opposed to organized religion in general—though they are not above organizing their own: it is the established Church which they resent.

There is no supra-conventional organization for witches, despite some attempts at "conventions" and the exceptional, highly legendary invoking of the Grand Coven for extraordinary tasks such as the repelling of the proposed Nazi invasion of England after Dunkirk. (English witches also claim to have kept Napoleon away.) Hierarchically, there is little differentiation among members of a coven; a novice is initiated after a probationary period of study, then advances through several grades, usually three, to become a genuine "priestess" (or "priest"). Each successful graduation is celebrated impressively, and somewhat more risqué in manner than in the Girl Scouts.

Theologically, witches claim to worship either a male or female divinity—often both, alternating both officiator and god semi-annually, in tune with the changing of the seasons from cold to hot, Celtic-fashion. This is supposedly based on paleolithic custom, since during the warm months a harvesting, gathering, matriarchal rule was more appropriate than during the cold winter months when male hunters had to take over . . . a neat but somewhat imaginary anthropology.

Some covens prefer a monotheistic cult of the Mother Goddess, known also as Artemis, Diana, Selene, and so on—fundamentally, a fertility-goddess identified with the moon, silver, the night, and the inner personality. The male counterpart is not a sun god, but the Horned God of the Hunt, the goat-headed fertility-god associated with Pan Priapus. The character of this nameless deity derives from a prehistorical sketch in the caves of southern France, but once again, the appeal to antiquity follows Margaret Murray's researches, *eventus ex vaticinione*. Most emphatic that their Horned God is no kin to the Christians' Devil, modern witchcraft devotees seem nonetheless aware that their god was in fact worshipped in that capacity by the thirteenth-century Luciferans and possibly by the Cathars, if the Inquisitor's reports can be believed. The "real" witches of the old European cults decidedly worshipped their horned visitor as Satan. Today the witches' cult seems to be a deliberate attempt to clear from their god's name any diabolical implications attached by history and the practice of modern satanists who also prefer horns on the Guest at their Black Masses and conjurations.

Few contemporary witches claim that their divinities are personal beings, but rather represent principles of life, love, fertility, and nature. The elaborate liturgies which they have created are enacted for their own sake as well as to "raise the power" latent in the human psyche. The possession of psychic abilities (ESP) is a cherished claim among many covenanters, and they also manifest glossolalia, healing, and (reportedly) levitation.

A typical liturgy begins with a "gathering"—an informal reception. When all are present, many (but not all) covens strip naked in order to free the powers within the members. A large circle, generally nine feet in diameter, is drawn, perhaps with a ritual sword or even chalk. The witches enter the circle of power, and the rite begins. This part of the ceremony is sometimes called "summoning the power," sometimes "drawing down the moon," although this variation (for some) involves only issues of great moment. The reason for the summoning may be as diverse as gaining love for a member, success in job-hunting, passing an exam, or healing a present or absent person. Dancing is employed to concentrate the members' energy, accompanied by chants, beating a drum, and invocations. The "cone of power"— the merged power of all—is raised and directed to its purpose. (Sometimes, among the black witches, the cone of power is said to become a deadly, malevolent force which can sicken or even kill.) The ritual is ended not by an unbridled orgy, but by a tea-party or the American equivalent: coffee and cake.

Secrecy is a normative influence among witches; not only do they shun publicity (with exceptions), but their instruments, books, and utensils are kept hidden from profane eyes. When a god is named, and many covens apparently have special divinities, the name is held secret from outsiders, lest its power be diminished. From the practices of the Golden Dawn, many of today's witches have borrowed the custom of having special names themselves, known only to the initiates. Such a use of names is truly of ancient magical origin; the name represents and somehow *is* the named.

Witches maintain that there are real benefits in belonging to a coven, apart from the solidarity of small-group identification (no small value in the technocratic society). Physical and mental cures, obtaining help or money, reclaiming lost property, finding solace are some of the valuable results of belonging. There is also the intense affirmation of humanistic purpose as well as the integrating factors that many of the young desire, who have found little comfort or reassurance in current church practice. Some young witches are former drug-users who have found in The Craft channels of mystical, personal adventure that have enabled them to forsake chemical ecstasy. There is a somewhat uncanny enthusiasm among witches for health foods, organic vegetables, and the like—perhaps not so uncanny, after all, considering the long-standing reliance on herbalism and folk medicine among the white witches.

Beyond the Mystery of Witchcraft

Belief in witches, replete with catalogues of their baneful works, have existed since man first scratched his mark on clay. Every land has its peculiar and timeless lore about demons, vampires, were-animals, magicians, and witches. Is it possible that all this is merest fantasy? that the centuries of laws, the horrible persecutions, the extant remains or images, talismans, grimoires, and the confessions are all fabricated on illusion? Yet how could all of it be true? And what of the extorted confessions, the lies, the intimidated, and false witnesses, the mania that still perdures as a brand on the conscience of the West, making modern "witch-hunts" equivalent to shameful and unjust persecution?

There is no simple answer. God alone—and perhaps the dead—know how much chicanery, madness, and true malice were blended with mere folk tales and fables to create the great fear. The one unalterable fact of its history is the vast obituary of those who witnessed to popular belief and fear with their blood.

Yet despite the horrors of the Inquisitions and the frenzied hunts of England, Scotland, and America, and even though thousands perished because of mere accusation or on the slimmest evidence, we must judge the past against the fact that belief in magic was nearly universal in all levels of society throughout the world until very recent times, and still exists in many lands. Further, scores of sorcerers and witches stoutly maintained to their last breath that they had indeed employed dark powers to murder, maim, and destroy. The additional fact of *their* victims' anguished deaths, although it can never mitigate the historical indictment against the persecutions, does make the great fear of sorcery and witchcraft more understandable.

Recent commentators on the race's strange fascination with the power of evil and the craft of witches find therein a symptom of a disease more profound and possibly more baneful—not indeed some incarnate god of iniquity, but rather a sickness in the body politic, a fault in the structure of society and culture. From a twenty-year study of African witchcraft and painstaking research into the history of the European variety, Geoffrey Parrinder suggests that a dramatic increase in witchcraft and its inevitable persecution, such as terrorized Nigeria as late as 1951, are an outgrowth of tensions and stresses caused by sudden changes in social values, cult, custom, technology, and so on. Such pressures, since they cannot be faced directly, invite the selection of a scapegoat on whom to ventilate civil or religious plaints. Witches, since they are by profession and personality rather antisocial, or at least the most disaffiliated group within the social system, are a particularly vulnerable target when the embers of fear and superstition are fanned by felt but unseen forces. In the early Middle Ages, as in Tsarist Russia and Hitler's Germany, the role of scapegoat fell similarly on the Jews, who perished no less horribly than did the witches. Eric Maple, another student of witchcraft, arrives at similar conclusions in his work *The Dark World of Witches*. How this process relates to the occult revolution will be taken up later on.

One of the dangling threads in any discussion of European witchcraft involves the origin of the beliefs and practices attributed to the witches and in some cases professed by them, such as flying, the Sabbath revels, the Black Mass, familiars, and so forth.

If the genuine witches did in fact anoint themselves before "flying" to a Sabbath with a salve concocted of materials indicated in extant formulas such as aconite and belladonna and other hallucinogenic agents, they could well have experienced in their delirium not only flight sensations but revels as wild and ostensibly real as the Sabbaths were to them. By simple autosuggestion, the beliefs they shared about such activities with their persecutors (who undoubtedly enlarged upon the accounts in good courtroom fashion) became their own fulfillment.

Animal familiars are not hard to account for, since solitary people (and real witches were almost always solitary) often keep pets on which they can lavish their unwanted or misplaced affection, the availability, size, and nature of the beasts being proportionate to the age and condition of their owner. Sad to say, such humble pets as dogs and cats, birds, mice, rabbits, and frogs were often executed in ways as fiendish as those devised for their masters. Sometimes they were merely exorcized and left to starve.

The Black Mass and the demonic agape were meticulously contrived forms of Catholic worship—in reverse, a logical outgrowth of the cult of dual divinities, whether real or imaginary. Thus the sorcerer or witch became the manifest but opposite counterpart of the priest, aping his gestures and intonations in mockery, although perhaps originally in deference to his "magic." Satanic cult was therefore easy to identify, but imperative to eradicate.

Thus, consciously or not, the Inquisition built on the vestiges of ancient rural magic a titanic straw-man which was systematically destroyed but always ready to return when need arose to divert popular discontent. The Black Mass, which will be considered at greater length in the following chapter, was, like witchcraft itself for the most part, a creature not of the devil but of the Inquisition.

That the Inquisition in all its creativity never persecuted witchcraft as anything but a Christian heresy and never as a pagan cult is of some significance considering the imaginative gifts of the investigators, but especially in light of modern claims of descent. Such assertions are reminiscent of Aryan myths of the Nazis and even less convincing. But they are important to those who make them because they weld a link with the ancient past and thus sanction the "restoration" of practices which are indeed ancient insofar as they correspond to some of the deepest religious needs of mankind: to be at one with nature and one's fellow man, to experience awe and wonder, to dance, sing, and celebrate in tune with the eternal rhythms of the race. Perhaps this is the real connection between ancient, medieval, and modern witchcraft—a frustrated longing for natural wholeness and festivity, awesome ceremony, and mystical union with transcendent reality, which is emerging in counter-cultural forms like a rose from thistles—a flower of dark and threatening aspect to the staid and unimaginative weeds.

7.

A Rumor of Devils

BAUDELAIRE's dictum, "The devil's cleverest wile is to persuade us that he doesn't exist," hardly applies to the alleged 7,000 members of the Church of Satan founded by Anton Szandor LaVey in the mid-sixties. LaVey, the "Black Pope," and his wife Diana are responsible for overseeing in a minimal capacity the twenty-five daughter "grottos" throughout the country. Most of the LaVeys' daily labors involve performing "satanic" weddings, funerals, and Black Masses—lest anyone get the impression that the Church of Satan is not a religion. A manual of black rituals and ceremonial curses was published by LaVey in 1970 under the title *The Satanic Bible*, a purple-covered paperback which achieved a sort of underground fame in short order, becoming a bestseller on college campuses in less than a year.

About the same time, even as Hell's Angels were playing Hun across the nation, a community of black-cloaked youngsters from London established themselves in New Orleans, Chicago, Boston, and other major urban centers. Following lights far different from those guiding the afficionados of LaVey's flashy California diabolism, these members of the Process Church of the Final Judgment ("Process People" for short) more resemble the Marcionites of the first century, praying to Satan, Lucifer, and Jehovah, avatars of the incomprehensible Supreme God now united in Christ.

Other types of satanism are more familiar to megalopolites: the Friday night double-feature horror thrillers on television,

Rosemary's Baby, a remake of *The Picture of Dorian Gray,* and the ever-present rumors of clandestine Black Masses being said in someone's living room or the basement of an abandoned church. Of course most of us would be somewhat embarrassed if we were seriously asked if we believed in Satan (as my students and I discovered), and perhaps the most strenuous objections to his reported existence come not from atheists and psychiatrists, but clergymen and theologians. Even Hell's Angels treat Lucifer more as a mascot than a divinity. But it might be less than a moot question to inquire whether a majority of people believe in demons than not, despite the obvious edge that professional skeptics enjoy in the press and pulpit. (An increasing number of religiously inclined persons, including Mr. LaVey, have recently wondered if modern theologians believe even in God.) Otherwise, why the sudden upswing in fashionable diabolism?

Satanism has obviously infiltrated contemporary culture and rather innocuously at that. Apart from films and novels (as in Blatty's *The Exorcist*), even the familiar peace-sign, that revitalized Winston Churchill victory emblem, has its basis in the ancient hand-sign against the evil-eye (as does the more vulgar nose-thumbing gesture). The occult revolution would seem a little tame if the devil were not given his due, and within a historical-sociological perspective, it would seem even stranger if satanism were not explicitly implicated. As with witchcraft, although there is no *necessary* connection between them, satanism has a long past and an interesting function within societies where it has made its secular appearance.

The Devil You Say

Demons of one or another kind have figured in folk theology since the beginning, perhaps in their earliest form as malevolent forces animating storms, floods, scorching winds, and disasters needing placation lest they destroy the people. Belief in man-hating spirits is as near a universal anthropological axiom as one could want and therefore it must have had some corresponding value for archaic and primitive mankind. Some of the earliest cuneiform texts are invocations against the malice of demons—the *Maskim* of Akkadia and Sumer. In Jewish folklore, Adam's first "wife" was the demon Lilith, who bore him monstrous offspring, according to Talmudic legends. Replaced by the gentler Eve, Lilith became a voracious night-hag, lurking in darkness to devour solitary travelers in the desert or to destroy children. Mesopotamian creation stories, such as the *Enuma Elish,* involve the god's slaying of a great, primeval dragon, possibly a crocodile —Leviathan, the spirit of chaos and darkness. In Persia, as early as the eighth century B.C., a well-developed theological dualism postulated two supreme gods, one good and the other evil, locked in an eternal struggle for domination. Zoroastrian Magism imported these beliefs into the Greek and Roman empires, where in the secret cults of Mithra, greatly favored by the military, their survival was assured well into the Christian era, influencing both East and West through Manichaeism and Catharism.

A widespread tenet of archaic and even contemporary religion is the existence of *incubi* and *succubi,* libidinous demons that seduce men and women in their sleep. Medieval lives of the saints and earlier stories are filled with tales about these licentious creatures who are, of course, successfully repelled. The attacks of these and similar demons are properly known as *obsession,* an unpleasant situation due to no fault of the afflicted and which involves no "interior" seizure or consent. Virtue itself may be the cause of such attacks, as in the Book of Job. The pranks of poltergeists (literally "noise-ghosts"), who throw furniture about and generally raise hell, fall into the same category spiritually. (Psychic investigators have more recently proposed that such phenomena result from a highly charged psychic "atmosphere" generated by people with great mental powers—although not necessarily intellectual gifts—such as the Curé d'Ars.)

A far more sinister demonic siege is *possession,* which involves the wholesale takeover of the victim's personality and body (although not his soul, necessarily) on a more or less permanent basis. Such tormented individuals are generally called demoniacs. Disease and madness were often ascribed to demonic possession, and ritual exorcisms were practiced in all ancient religions from Tibet to Mexico. Early Christians took such beliefs as seriously as anyone else, and until 1971 the Church promotes its clerical candidates to the rank of exorcist before ordination to the priesthood, although the exercise of this power is left to the discretion of the local bishop (excepting the "ordinary" exorcisms incorporated until recently in baptismal rites and Easter services). The Anglican clergy, Protestant ministers, Jewish rabbis, and other religious leaders perform similar supernatural operations for the benefit of their flocks. It might be said that psychiatrists do likewise, but the fee is greater and the process longer.

According to the Gospels, Jesus and his disciples performed exorcisms of various kinds, sometimes by a word of command though in other cases they had to resort to "prayer and fasting." In the New Testament, possession and obsession are chief characteristics of demons, and even in Revelations—the most heterodox of Christian scriptural works—the spirit of the Evil One speaks and acts through his minions, persecuting the Church rather than luring the faithful into secret sins. Such accounts, which do not assert but presuppose the existence of demons and diabolical phenomena, have caused theologians from Wreimarus in the eighteenth century right up to the Bultmannians' demythologization purges, to reinterpret Scripture in the light of "modern" science, which refuses to tolerate miracles, demons, angels, and their ilk. Such a policy has met with great opposition, not only among the faithful, but also from psychologists and philosophers such as Karl Jaspers and Carl G. Jung.

In truth, primitive Christian belief in demons was a shared characteristic of most peoples in the Mediterranean world at that time. But the strange profile of the demythologized Gospel has caused many to wonder if the attempt to exorcize (literally) these cultural elements of early Christian theology is really less drastic than allowing them to remain. In terms of the occult revolution, an increasing number of people seem more comfortable with the demons than with the theologians. In America, England, and France, religious exorcisms are evidently on the increase, and certainly in Latin America, the Indies, and Africa they are as common as ever. The demonic has evident meaning for many Christians and other religious people today. Attempts to exorcize the Justice Department and the Pentagon may, however, imply a subtle redefinition of demonic possession in the minds of the younger generation.

Pagan mystics such as Apollonius of Tyana, as well as the Jewish rabbis of antiquity and the Middle Ages, the Christian Fathers and Doctors, and priests and witchdoctors in every age and land have all worked to retrench demonic power in the world, often with tragic results. Terrible persecutions of reputed witches and sorcerers, such as that which convulsed Nigeria in 1951, are but one consequence of an exaggerated emphasis on the power of evil spirits. Another is the sad fact that hundreds of thousands of people have, as a result of belief in demons and their human agents, spent the greater portion of their lives in conscious fear of being ravaged by some horrible minion of hell. Christian preachers, among whom the Mathers and Jonathan Edwards must rank supreme, discovered that threats and descriptions of hell and the ever-ready attacks of evil spirits were a tempting and potent device for controlling their flocks. Even the Wesleys were somewhat inclined towards the appeal to the demonic to inspire their congregations with holy terror.

Long before the Reformers, however, demons had been important members in the supernatural cast of Christian tradition.

Necromancers—those who summon the spirits of the dead to discover from them the shape of things to come—were also thought to call up demons and to achieve their visions by demonic power. At the beginning of the third century of the Christian era, the Alexandrian theologian Origen simply declared that "the associates of magicians are apostate and evil spirits and foul demons." St. Anthony of Egypt, like Jesus, was sorely tried in the desert by demons anxious to subvert his austere manner of life. Undaunted, he went on to father Christian monasticism. For centuries, pagan divinities were identified with demons, even from the time of Paul, and in the early fifth century Augustine still identified the nymphs and fauns of legends and myths with the incubi and succubi of Persian demonology. He forthrightly condemned demonic pacts and consultations with magicians. His irascible contemporary, Jerome, although less severe in his judgment of magicians, was nonetheless a firm believer in the malevolent conspiracies of demons.

During the next five hundred years, little was added (or subtracted) from Christian demonology. More importantly, Satan himself, the personal devil, would not appear on the religious stage until the Middle Ages when, as in the case of witchcraft, he emerges in a novel form and role.

The Adversary

Belief in a personal evil spirit of great and even divine power is a fairly late development in Judaeo-Christian theology. But the roots of this belief trail back to the deserts and plains of ancient Mesopotamia. One of the earliest references to a malevolent spirit is in the Book of Job, much of which derives from non-Jewish sources and reflects the theogonies of peoples such as the Canaanites and Babylonians. In Job, this personage is portrayed as one of the Lord's ministers, whose duty it is to test human fidelity. Hence his title: *Shaitan,* "Adversary," which is transliterated into our English name "Satan," although it was never properly a name at all. In Greek, the satan became *"diabolos,"* a current rendering of the legal nuance, for his Greek name signifies an accuser, which was the role of Job's *shaitan* among the jurors of the heavenly assizes. From *"diabolos,"* which literally means "one who throws against," come our English words "diabolic" and "devil." We easily think of *the* Devil as a supreme malevolent spirit whose name is Satan, but neither word appears in the Old Testament as a proper name except for a single instance in 1 Chronicles 21, 1, which is a retelling of David's census, differing from 2 Samuel 24, 1 only in identifying the wicked scheme with the counsel of "Adversary" rather than that of the Lord. (In earlier Jewish thought, all that befell mankind came from the Lord alone, whether good or ill; only in conscious contrast with Persian dualistic thought did it become necessary to dichotomize and reify the source of weal and woe, lest the Lord God be identified with the evil deity of Zoroastrianism.)

If there was no proper devil as such, there were plenty of demons in ancient Hebrew thought, dwelling in the desert, the "lower air," around cemeteries, tombs, and the like. But these creatures, who were decidedly under God's rule and bane, were not the minions of any arch-fiend. Nor were Leviathan and Behemoth, those primeval monsters of Mesopotamian legend who were adopted straightway into Job. These beasts were, rather, God's playthings—a great crocodile and the hippopotamus, somewhat unusual pets to be sure, but proof that God was in command and that his ways were transcendentally strange.

Lucifer, a name which first appears in Jerome's translation of Isaiah (14, 12–15), was used merely as a poetic comparison of the King of Babylon to the morning star, Venus, the last and most beautiful star to fade before the blazing dawn. The Greeks called it *"phosphoros,"* the Romans *"lucifer,"* both names meaning "lightbearer," perhaps because Venus's appearance meant the approach of the sun. In Hebrew the same name was rendered *helel ben shahar,*" "day star, son of the morning." Thus, by equating the despised Babylonian with the proud star of morning which was eclipsed by the brilliance of the sun (God), Isaiah was also laying the foundation for a poetic demonology, for we read in the apocryphal Book of Enoch how Azazel, head of the fallen spirits, was like a "star fallen from heaven." In St. Luke's gospel (10, 18), Jesus speaks of Satan "falling like lightning from heaven." In Revelations (12, 4), the great dragon drags down a third of the stars, an allusion perhaps to the Book of Daniel (8, 10), where it was possibly an original reference to the arrogance of Alexander the Great.

Other legends about demons slowly added to the growing personification of the devil. In Genesis 6 there is a strange story of the *Nephilim,* the giants of old begotten by the "Sons of God" of the "Daughters of Men." These "Sons of God" were later thought to be angels who, envious of man's physical body, also lusted after Adam's daughters. According to the apocryphal 1 Enoch, these "Watchers" aligned themselves with the defiant "Lucifer" and with him were cast out of heaven by Michael and the faithful angels, a legend repeated in Revelation (12, 7–9). Another demonic personality from the Old Testament was Asmodeus, the lustful and murderous devil of Tobit (4, 25), who was later bound in the Egyptian desert by Raphael, one of the seven spirits who stand in the presence of God. Furthermore, like the later Christian theologians, the Jewish prophets often ridiculed pagan divinities by identifying them with demons, thus, for instance, creating Beelzebub ("Lord of the Flies") from *Ba'al zebul,* a Canaanite god who was worshipped in Ekron in the days of Ahaz and whose name originally meant "Lord, the Prince" before Elijah got hold of it (2 Kings 1, 4).

During the intertestamental period, when the great apocalyptic books such as Enoch, the Testament of the Twelve Patriarchs, the Lives of Adam and Eve, Esdras, and others were written to encourage the Jews in their struggle to preserve their faith in the midst of Hellenistic persecution and cultural attrition, the theology of evil developed into a complex demonology that has influenced Jewish and Christian thought ever since. Such works, especially 1 Enoch and the Assumption of Moses, were alluded to or even quoted in the canonical epistles of Peter and Jude. The Dead Sea Scrolls and other writings of the Essenes, as well as the canonical Revelation of John, were heavily influenced by these allegorical romances, which unabashedly personified kings, emperors, pagan gods, and apostates as monstrous demons—dragons, beasts, were-animals, and the like. Central to their message is that opposition to the kingdom of God is due to the undying enmity of the Evil One, but that God will ultimately prevail.

By the first century, then, the Adversary had gained a composite personality, as is evident in Revelation; he is partly the serpent of Eden, Leviathan, the Watcher's Azazel, Lucifer, Job's *Shaitan,* Beelzebub, Asmodeus, the "lion," and probably much more. He is also definitely in command; in Revelation the only other named devil, Abaddon ("*Appolyon*" in Greek) is a subordinate to the dragon, Satan (9, 12).

These rudiments were subsequently developed by Jewish, Christian, and Islamic theologians towards ever further detail, as they multiplied the fallen angels into the millions, carefully arranged in military ranks under the supreme commander. Thus Michael and his legions stood against Satan (or Lucifer) and his hordes, including his generals: Beelzebub, Asmodeus, Astorath, Abaddon, Sataniel, Lucifuge, Acheron, and many, many more. Like the dual deities of ancient Zoroastrianism, these "celestial" armies were locked in lasting battle, but one that would eventually see the triumph of the good. Such notions, mingled with the folklore and superstitions of gentile and pagan peoples (whose former gods were added to the ranks of the demons—or the angels, depending on the point of view, became the caliginous inheritance of medieval Christendom: a vast, fascinating theology of Satan.

The Horned God

The apocalyptic fright of the tenth century added a new depth to the old terror of Satan and his army, mankind's immortal enemies whose temporary reign, prelude to the final battle, was feared might begin with the changing of the millennium, a belief based on passages in Revelation (20, 3, 7–10). Such fears induced preachers and theologians further to enlarge their already ample demonologies. Gratian argued in the twelfth century that since demons loved blood (Lilith?), then necromancers must use human blood in their ritual conjurations to summon demons. (So loathesome were these demons that they were coerced into appearing in "pleasing" shape, lest their real appearance kill the beholder.) The great Jewish theologian Moses ben Maimon (Maimonides) described the wiles and practices of the desert spirits, while William of Paris wrote convincingly of satanic cults in which the devil appeared to his devotees in the form of a huge, black cat.

There were those who actually worshipped the powerful spirit of evil (as there are today), for the extant grimoires (Latin: "*grimoria,*" the "black books") of medieval magicians are filled with references to conjurations, pacts, promises, and the ready availability of demonic power for those whose daring was greater than their alchemical skill. More tragically, devil worship was identified with the Cathars, witches, and Templars, as we have seen, and Jews were, of course, always suspect of such dealings. A medieval treatise known as the *Errores Haereticorum* went so far as to claim that the very name Cathar came from the word cat, an animal "whose posterior they kiss, in whose form Satan appears to them." (The Latin word for cat was "*catus,*" but the Cathars took their name, which meant the "pure ones," from the

Greek *"catharos,"* "pure." Such specious etymologies were acceptable evidence in the Middle Ages, and an unbreakable link was forged between cats, devils, and heretics, including witches.) The Cathars were also first to ride brooms to their meetings, which were derisively called "Synagogues of Satan" by anti-Semitic Christians, and that interesting skill also rubbed off on the witches.

As the Cathars' assemblies and the witches' Sabbaths merged in the demonologies of medieval churchmen, it was a matter of course that the devil would become a regular visitor to the Sabbaths. As we related earlier, he changed his appearance from that of a cat to a goat for that purpose, which has some connection with the scapegoat offered by the ancient Jews to Azazel on the Day of Atonement as well as to the possible allusion to the pagan gods Pan and Cernunos. But a horned, tailed, hoofed, and hairy Satan became the common image. (His bat-wings were perhaps the imaginary opposite of angels' wings, which were feathery; bats, like cats, although far less vicious creatures, have had a very bad press among theologians. Why bats are associated with evil is strictly a matter of conjecture—perhaps for their nocturnal preference and peculiar sleeping habits. Vampire bats were unknown to the ancient world.)

While "black" magicians, the Luciferans of the thirteenth century, and the strange "Brethren of the Cross" in Thuringia as late as the sixteenth century did actually worship Satan, and it is even possible that the Templars' Baphomet was the devil, it is highly unlikely that witches were involved in Satanism until the fifteenth century when, perhaps out of spite or believing that the devil alone could offer them any protection against the fury of the Church, they deliberately fulfilled the expectations of the Inquisition.

The Black Mass

Besides the righteous attempt to eradicate devilish witchcraft, a further characteristic of medieval belief in Satan was the gradual emergence of the Black Mass. Among the earliest accounts of witches' Sabbaths, there are only the vaguest references to sacrilegious rites, although the Luciferans and Waldensians did mock the Catholic sacraments. Once again, the mere likelihood that such emissaries of Satan could parody Christian ritual meant that witches would eventually be accused of it as well, and by the sixteenth century ritual sacrilege had become one of the prime accusations against them. By the curious dialectics of the self-fulfilling prophecy, what started as a suspicion in the minds of the Inquisitors eventually became a "fact" not only in the minds of the crowds who taunted the agonized victims in their death throes, but in some cases the actual practice of witches.

Many accounts of Black Masses are extant, many of them no doubt spurious, but a semi-authentic (if melodramatic) recreation can be heard on the album *Witchcraft* recorded by an on-putting Chicago rock group who call themselves "The Coven." Basically, the ritual represents a deliberate inversion of the Catholic Mass, involving black candles, reversed symbols and gestures, and conscious profanation of the host which, in former times had to be consecrated by a defrocked priest or stolen from a Catholic Church, thus inviting a reciprocal enlargement of the Church's paranoia and subsequent investigations—an early instance of escalation. (One of Graham Greene's best short stories, "The Hint of an Explanation," revolves about a plot to steal a host.) Slowly, these perverted rites grew to truly hideous proportions, even to ritual murder and incredible sexual pathology.

Among the more famous Satanists of history were Gilles de Laval and Madame de Montespan. The former, a marshal of France, Baron of Retz, and the prototype of the Bluebeard stories, was burned alive at Nantes in 1440 for the murder of two hun-

132

dred children from the district of Tiffauges. These victims, according to somewhat reputable accounts, were needed for the satanic Masses and other horrors which Laval and his associates performed. He is said to have been apprehended in the act of slaughtering five children from Nantes. Riots had previously broken out as grieved parents sought recourse, their appeals attracting the attention of John V, Duke of Brittany. His investigators unearthed the Baron's ghastly cult, which included several churchmen. Doubtless the macabre details of these events were amplified by their chroniclers, but the exploits of Madame de Montespan two centuries later are far more susceptible of historical confirmation.

During the seventeenth century, sacrilegious Masses were so rife in France that Louis XIV established a secret court to hear cases involving so explosive an issue. Called the Chambre Ardente (the "burning court"), it was placed under the jurisdiction of the Police Commissioner of Paris, who quite accidentally turned up the evidence that eventuated in the apprehension of Madame de Montespan's associates.

One of Louis' mistresses, Madame de Montespan rose to that high position by the adroit use of magic, by which she believed she could win and maintain the favor of the king. As Louis was notoriously fickle, when Madame de Montespan's star began to set, she increased the dosage of Black Masses, even to the point of sacrificing stolen infants. For this purpose, she had enlisted the aid of Catherine Deshayes, a fortune-teller, and several abbés. Failing in her attempts to keep Louis' favor, Madame de Montespan was resolved to poison him before she was too much eclipsed. Again, however, repeating the events of Tiffauges centuries before, the frantic parents of the abducted Parisian children rioted and an investigation was begun. La Voison, as Catherine Deshayes was called, was soon arrested, convicted, and sentenced to death. She was burned alive in 1680. Shortly thereafter, the police literally stumbled across evidence that eventually implicated Madame de Montespan. The lady was not for burning, however, and her part in the horrors was not made public until after her death. Needless to say, her days at court were neither many nor happy; she retired to a convent, where she ended her days in solitude and prayer. The Burning Court was suppressed in 1680, although by Louis' command its investigations continued in secret for two more years.

Saying the Mass for utilitarian purposes, whether evil or not, is a magical practice of some antiquity; in 694 the Council of Toledo forbade Masses for the Dead being said for living persons, which was supposed to bring about their death. The "custom" nevertheless perdured, appearing in records from 1220, and as late as 1500 an ecclesiastical dispute between the Bishop of Cambrais and his Chapter involved hostile imprecations being incorporated into a Mass said by the Dean of the Cathedral. In 1525 Paulus Grimaldus condemned such practices as criminal offenses.

Black magicians found in the Mass a potent weapon for their supernatural armory, for it was the apex of Catholic religious cult, the words of transsubstantiation being considered preeminently powerful. Apparently, the "magical" words *"hocus pocus"* are a bowdlerized echo of the *"Hoc est corpus meum"* of the consecratory prayer. Likewise, in an age of superstitious fear, "votive" Masses easily degenerated into magical exercises. As far back as the ninth century, Pope Nicholas I had cause to outlaw the Mass of Judgment which was said to assure the conviction or acquittal of an accused criminal. But Masses continued to be said for rain or fair weather, to obtain children or abundant crops, to ward off animal diseases, to prevent plague, famine, and the attacks of enemies, to gain someone's love, to assure a safe journey in this world or to the next one, to obtain buried treasure or the gift of tears. (A few votive Masses are still found in the back of missals, but their use has steadily declined since the Second Vatican Council.)

Abuses of Christian cult help explain not only the development of the Black Mass but also the hostility with which many Protestant reformers viewed Catholic ritual. And although magical Masses continued underground, in Protestant nations magical rites and even witches' Sabbaths soon began to resemble prayer meetings, down to the sedentary presence of the "man in black," the ex-Goat of Mendes who now had donned Calvinist or Methodist robes.

Satanism prospered secretly in eighteenth-century England and France, even during the heyday of deism and atheism, although it cannot be said to have ever amounted to much. Hellfire Clubs were the rage among some of the hot-blooded young nobility of London and Dublin around 1730, and the name of Sir Francis Dashwood has been linked since that time with diabolical orgies, human sacrifice, and devil worship. The Marquis de Sade included a lengthy description of a Gallic Black Mass in *Justine,* and Huysmans echoed him a century later in *Là-Bas.*

But by the nineteenth century, at least in popular imagination, the Black Mass had become the chief stock-in-trade of satanists and magicians, and it was mentioned in the writings of Eliphas Levi and later in the extensive works of those marvelous magicians Macgregor Mathers and Aleister Crowley, who waged a sort of unholy war for control of the occult Order of the Golden Dawn. Crowley, who prided himself on flamboyant anti-Christian antics, calling himself "The Great Beast," "666," and "The Wickedest Man Alive," is (erroneously) believed to have composed and celebrated Black Masses, an idea he probably planted himself. (An international scoundrel, heroin addict, adventurer, novelist, and student of the occult, Crowley was expelled from France and Italy and was merely tolerated in his native England.)

Victorian diabolism was not only a British foible, however. In 1895, three years before the young Crowley joined the Order of the Golden Dawn, a satanic chapel was discovered in Rome's

Borghese palace, a hidden room sumptuously decorated with infernal emblems and icons.

Throughout the present century, newspaper accounts from practically every European and American nation have reported on occasion that a Black Mass or similar festival has been performed in a deserted church or graveyard, in warehouses and brownstone flats and chic penthouses overlooking the East River. There is little doubt that such things really occur; several college students of my acquaintance have mentioned at least hearing of such goings-on even in frat houses and dormitories. However, today's Black Mass, a literary invention in the first place, is a fairly mild version of the infanticidal orgies of Gilles de Laval and Madame de Montespan. Even in California, mecca of the unorthodox in religious cult, there is little evidence of real sacrilege—stealing a host from a Catholic Church just doesn't have the thrill it once did.

Satanic rites are not restricted to the Black Mass, and to discount contemporary diabolism as a lot of harmless fun would be as fatuous as to find in it evidence of utter corruption in society and a threat to God and country. The blossoming of evil is never pretty, whether in the jungles of Vietnam or in the ritual sacrifice of brute beasts in demonic cults. Although some contemporary cults associated with demonic emphasis, such as the Process Church, are vehemently anti-vivisectionist, other less positive sects have taken to animal sacrifice to express their "ancient" lineage. Human sacrifice is not out of the question; several murders, particularly the Tate-LaBianca and Ohta cases, have been linked to this morbid aspect of the occult revolution. Drugs figure prominently in some cults and are rigidly prohibited by others—again, the Process Church comes to mind. Sexual "abandon" may or may not be involved, although the far-out cults seem to indulge in several varieties of sado-masochistic rites which sometimes result in physical injury.

Voodoo is becoming more common in many southern and

southwestern states along with necromancy and even vampirism, if one is to believe newspaper accounts. The Chicago *Daily News* featured a story not so long ago of a Houston housewife who was driven to near hysteria when she discovered on her front porch a large jar containing a dog fetus and a frog, which were to have made her sterile. New York and New Orleans have flourishing voodoo and obeah cults.

The Church of Satan

In comparison to the other varieties of satanic practice, Anton LaVey's Church of Satan begins to look somewhat tame, despite the inclusion of his own Black Mass and scary mumbo-jumbo. A "missal" section is contained in his *Satanic Bible,* but the liturgy is comparatively innocuous. LaVey is sufficiently wary to avoid a public parody of the Mass even today, not perhaps so much because it would result in any great hue and cry, but rather because the Vatican Council has engendered so many changes in the Mass itself that a parody would hardly be recognizable. LaVey does not hesitate to mock psycho-dramatics and encounter groups, however, which he associates with the Black Mass, and which if nothing else suggests the religious significance of modern psychological enthusiasm.

Not about to be caught on the wrong side of the sacred canopy, however, LaVey has enough archaic symbols and artifacts strewn about to satisfy the longings of the most outraged old-style Catholic: swords, aspergilla, bells, candles, incense, incantations, and even parchment paper. Although he admits to practicing magic, and despite wholesale borrowing from witchcraft ceremonial, LaVey is not a witch and most contemporary witches stay well away from the Church of Satan. LaVey's magic is more of a gimmick, a device to stimulate the release of sexual energy and whatever else wants releasing in the LaVeyan way—anger, lust, greed, pride, vengeance—than it is a form of worship.

In all, "Dr." Anton LaVey seems a bit reminiscent of John Wel-lington Wells, Gilbert and Sullivan's sorcerer, than he resembles Cagliostro or Eliphas Levi. And for good reason: his fascinating career before he became the "Exarch of Hell" included lion-taming, palm-reading, and playing the calliope in Clyde Beatty's circus. He was also a police photographer. It is not insignificant that among those to whom the *Satanic Bible* is dedicated appears the name of Phineas Taylor Barnum.

Nevertheless, it would be far off the mark to assume that LaVey is nothing more than a carnival barker in a devil suit. His little book, as an indictment of contemporary Christianity, is not all circus fire-and-brimstone; young people have much to begrudge the organized churches, and LaVey has a gift of putting their frustrations into forceful prose: "With all of the contra-dictions in the Christian scriptures, many people currently cannot rationally accept Christianity the way it has been practiced in the past. Great numbers of people are beginning to doubt the existence of God, in the established Christian sense of the word. So, they have taken to calling themselves 'Christian Atheists.' True, the Christian Bible is a mass of contradictions; but what could be more contradictory than the term 'Christian Atheist'?"[1]

It is not necessary to take LaVey seriously (although many do) to see in his lengthy critique of practiced Christianity the merit of at least partial accuracy. And for all the cant, there is a sort of fascinating honesty about a "religion" that unhypocritically endorses lust, revenge, hatred, greed, and other "capital" sins officially but not always privately eschewed by churchgoers.

New Notes from the Underground: The Process Church

Far removed from Anton LaVey's exotically devilish parlor games is the Process Church of the Final Judgment. Its members' black cloaks, long hair, occasional beards, and especially their

---

[1] *The Satanic Bible,* page 43.

addition of Satan and Lucifer to Jehovah and Christ as the "four gods of the universe," can easily give the impression that this youthful religious community enrolls hippie satanists in the grand tradition of Crowley and LaVey. Nothing could be less true. These "Processeans" are thoroughly counter-cultural in their religious and communitarian life-style, but they can be called "occult" in only a very technical sense: they actively shun the public limelight, quite unlike LaVey and more in tune with witchcraft. There is no trace of magic or witchcraft among them, however, and their ritual bears no resemblance to a Black Mass (or any other recognizable rite). The popular notion of occultism characterizes the Process Church of the Final Judgment about as much as it does the ACLU. In fact, there is a strong emphasis on a psychological interpretation of the forces at work in the universe rather than a reliance on the mythical anthropomorphism typical of LaVey's explanations of the role of Satan. Process methodology would do credit to many a liberal theologian in the more orthodox tradition of Christianity.

One of the more interesting aspects of their creed merits a brief comment in context of the occult revolution, however: the assertion that the end of the world is near. While not an original contribution, Processean eschatology is rather unlike the preachments of Seventh Day Adventists and Jehovah's Witnesses or, for that matter, the Children of God. Processeans believe that the world has been geared for self-destruction by human engineering. To be sure, there is a good chance that someone may push the final button one day soon whether by conscious design, madness, or stupidity (or any combination of the three)—and even the possibility of an "accident" has been probed on a popular level by the media. Among films of recent vintage which have added to contemporary eschatological feeling, there are *Fail Safe, The Bedford Incident,* and *On the Beach,* and Stanley Kubrick's *Dr. Strangelove* still ranks as one of the great artistic statements about human folly in the face of the absurd struggle for nuclear supremacy in the modern world. *War Game* had a devastatingly apocalyptic impact on those who saw it, and more recently the *Planet of the Apes* and its sequels served to remind us of our precarious position vis-à-vis The Bomb and other technological gadgets. *The Andromeda Strain* extended the specter from the military to the merely scientific, without the incredible excesses of most science-fiction films, touching again the eschatological nerve that recent ecological doom-sayers have so thoroughly tenderized. We have learned from them that Armageddon is now in the very air we breathe and in the DDT and mercury accumulating in our tissues, in the poison flowing from our faucets and the uncontrolled over-population of the planet.

Consequently, it is not surprising to find similar allusions in the theology of the Process Church of the Final Judgment, where psychology has blended so well with current social themes. Like the early Christians, however, the Processeans happily anticipate the End, for in that transformation of human consciousness will occur, they believe, the destruction of inner and outer repression and the triumphant liberation of love.

There is a definite evangelistic tendency in the group, and public witness is an integral component of their commitment. Even in street encounters, the Processeans reveal themselves to be warmly engaging rather than polemic and dour, and the fruits of their labors and demeanor is evident in the numbers of interested young men and women they are attracting.

Organizationally, the Church is an international movement. Begun in London in 1963, the original Processeans migrated to Mexico and then to the United States, where they established themselves in New Orleans, Chicago, San Francisco, Boston, and north as far as Toronto. The leaders of the Chicago group are British, but the composition of the community is ethnically eclectic. There is no question about the structure of the group, however; a definite hierarchical order exists and good discipline is manifest. Still, the spirit of the group is anything but rigid and there is no taint of authoritarianism. The obvious charisma of the leaders is perhaps the reason; they stand out as gifted, articulate, and self-confident exponents of an attractive way of life. Their authority is earned, not imposed.

While obviously opposed in principle to the organized churches, a rejection which finds expression in the clothes, liturgy, theology, and structure of the group, the Process Church is not antagonistic towards other denominations. There are a few satirical references to the major religions of Western culture in the only issue of *Process* (the Church's magazine) that I have seen, but the comic parody of the Judaeo-Christian establishment is certainly much less shrill than LaVey's invective and even some of the criticism coming from within the ranks of "orthodoxy."

As an episode of the occult revolution, the emergence of the Process Church of the Final Judgment is a happy omen that a band of religiously committed young men and women endeavoring to discover value and meaning in a world programmed for self-destruction and courageously proclaiming their vision of liberation and love can pull it off with grace and wit in the streets of Babylon.

The Demonic Element

Belief in demons is part of mankind's nursery furniture, perhaps a necessary part considering the possibility of a total moral shock from a realization of full human responsibility for the horrors we have perpetrated upon each other from the beginning. Yet the devil as he is popularly conceived is a creation of the Middle Ages. Medieval demonology was not merely a character sketch of a cosmic villain, however, but a thorough-going social system composed of grades of service, roles, areas of competence, and accountabilities divided among a host of hierarchically arranged personnel. In this, demonology was merely a negative image of medieval angelology, which made for symmetry and did its share to explain such events as the Black Death, famine, and war.

In a society on the verge of chaos—apparently meaningless disasters, very real horrors of war and brutality, grinding poverty, and the oppressiveness of Church and king—inexplicable but dread events such as earthquakes, tidal waves, cyclones, and volcanic eruptions could all be traced to a definite source against which some action could be taken. Such possibilities included exorcisms, prayers for deliverance, expiation by self-discipline—the scourge or the pilgrimage, or occasionally placating the evil spirit directly if nothing better worked, even to the point of serving and worshipping him, as in the legend of St. Christopher. Feudal allegiance went to the most powerful protector as a matter of course.

More likely, the devil could be persecuted vicariously in the person of his votaries, such as witches and sorcerers, the existence of whom was therefore a social necessity, and there were usually a few deviant groups around who would serve in a pinch—"If all else fails, blame the Jews." Whatever the form of satanic belief, it served to focus the fears and anxieties of common folk onto an identifiable target, a psycho-social surrogate, which theologians and preachers seemed only too eager to adorn with ever more elaborately sinister characteristics. Like witchcraft, devil-worship was in most cases the creature of Christian superstition and need for a scapegoat to take away the sins of the world. The survival of both factors to this day is perhaps wholly due to the success of the Inquisition in reifying the imaginary object of their quest, thus falling victim to the self-fulfilling prophecy. Today elements of such tendencies are still evident in the hostile attacks on America's young dissenters by reactionary politicians, a process which reached a tragic climax with the incidents at Kent State and Jackson, Mississippi.

Although there has been little previous overt supernaturalism among collegians before 1970, Theodore Roszak had sniffed the drift towards youthful counter-cultural occultism as early as 1968, following the spoor back to the miasmal social swamps from which they were in headlong flight. In the Slough of Despond that had once been passed off as the Great Society, Roszak found the masters of destiny employed in antiseptic word-games behind which the grim horror of war was effectively camouflaged and the brutal exploitation of the powerless poor was disguised as social improvement.

The Explanation of a Hint

From the remote origins of satanism in Persian dualism and the Jewish attempts to account for evil, Western thought passed through a veritable valley of the shadow of death, the figure of His Satanic Majesty looming ever larger in men's imaginations. The proud and tragic figure of Lucifer in Milton's *Paradise Lost* surely represents the apotheosis of personified evil, a vastly different character from the demons of the Gospels. Today, few believe in a personal devil, although the mystery of evil still haunts the consciences of us all. And we are no doubt as prone as were our ancestors to focus our fears and concretize them, ever anxious for a scapegoat who will once again prove to us our own guiltlessness.

Demons there may be, but wickedness springs first from within man himself. No greater remedy for the devil mania exists than the conviction of personal sinfulness. Our contemporary attempts to reify the source of the myriad disasters and tragedies of life, producing "evil spirits" behind every bush and new ideology, are, as they always were, an escape from confronting the challenges of historical existence with all the attendant risks of failure through personal weakness, ignorance, and malice. The demonic is ourselves, and this is the meaning perhaps of the attempted redemption of Satan and Lucifer in the Process Church and Anton LaVey's Church of Satan.

As demons in general provide a concrete surrogate for the evil in man's heart as he flees from the challenges and consequences of mortal life, so do specific devils come to be seen as manifestations of particular fears and taboos. Incubi and succubi, the sexual molesters, are reified fears of sexual responsibility. Even in the Middle Ages, obsessed wives sometimes refused to be exorcized, so enamored had they become of their spirit-lovers. ("Inexplicable" pregnancies and other inconveniences of marital infidelity could also be laid to the "attacks" of such demons, thus rendering them the more valuable.) Other forms of demonic siege, obsession, and possession can be partially explained by psychosomatic abilities and suggestibility latent in everyone. This does not, of course, lessen the severity of the assaults, but at least helps explain why exorcism really works. It is sufficient to believe in the power of the exorcist, perhaps whether or not he does so himself, or even whether or not he believes in demons.

Extreme reductionism is as vapid as excessive credulity, and I do not mean to assert that demons do not exist—rather, their existence is evident and manifold, simultaneously transcending physical limits and having enormous power. The demonic principality is primarily in man and his society, however, and its power is real; perhaps human malevolence can be somehow materialized and "intelligent" in this universe as well. The potential of the human mind and spirit are still unknown. But to transfer the source of moral evil, to project it to "other" spheres of existence, is to cultivate inauthenticity and is therefore radically anti-Christian. Needless to add, the sheer pressure of contemporary life inclines us to do just that.

The root causes of the horrors of our world, from Auschwitz to Son My and Altamont, seem strangely invisible and certainly beyond the control and understanding of ordinary citizens. Also the churches have often defaulted in their role of prophetic witness, retaining only the outer formalities of ritual and administration. Not surprisingly, lay membership and attendance have dropped off ever more sharply in recent years, even as ministers, priests, and nuns have renounced their professional commitment in increasing numbers. The "sacred canopy" has been rent asunder, and there above our heads loom the forces of chaos and absurdity. Although it cannot halt the deterioration of religious systems and structures, the rebirth in our time of the appreciation of the demonic *in man* may forestall the frantic search for scapegoats, which typically results from a sudden collapse of conventional cultural and moral norms. In the lurch of the technological revolution, as the future bursts on us so frighteningly, the present generation experiences the full force of such a deterioration of values.

In the Process Church, even among Anton LaVey's sectaries, there is the promise of hope, for in both are recognized—in consonance with Christian tradition—that evil does not stem from beyond man's own world: "What goes into the mouth does not defile a man; but it is what comes out of the mouth that defiles a man" (Mt. 15, 11).

8.

Divination and the Future

WILLIAM FULD's name is almost unknown, yet his influence has been greater than that of most statesmen, scientists, and clergymen, for it was he who presented to the world that mysterious contraption called the ouija board. Building on a hoary foundation of magical tradition, the planchette and circle of letters, Fuld marketed his "device" (as the present copyright owners, Parker Brothers, Incorporated, now deem it) in the 1890's. A perennial success, now surpassing even *Monopoly,* the ouija board is possibly the most widely played parlor "game" in America. (The occult-sounding name, incidentally, is simply a combination of the French and German words for "yes.") Having made a striking comeback recently after a slight decline during the halcyon Eisenhower years, it is perhaps. appropriate to recall that ouija board sales tend to follow the curve of political, natural, and social disasters and crises—the First World War and the Depression were, for instance, peak sales periods. Actually, interest in all forms of occultism, and not only semi-necromantic devices such as the ouija board, increases in war-time and depressed periods, just as religious observance and church attendance picks up. The present decline in the latter is, therefore, of serious importance in view of the present world and national situation and the undeniable re-emergence of occultism.

Fuld's ouija board is by no means the only form of divination popular in America today—although its commercial history is the longest; various editions of the ancient Chinese book of oracles, the *I Ching*, are outselling Freud and Darwin. Tarot decks are more common on college campuses and in the suburbs than are "regular" playing cards. There seems to be a run on crystal balls, and books dealing with almost every aspect of the subject chase each other from the shelves of drugstores and book-dealers. More "classical" forms of divination are still popular among the older generation from tea-leaf reading to seances.

While a rather minor part of the occult revolution compared to the drama of witchcraft and satanism, divination of various sorts, especially Tarot reading and palmistry, is becoming more popular in the counter culture as is the ouija board. That clues in the murder case of Dr. Victor Ohta and his family involved the Tarot cards should serve to remind us, however, that even this somewhat subordinate area of contemporary occultism is not without its sinister side. During the patristic period and the Middle Ages, divination was indeed singled out for attack by Christian theologians as being particularly dangerous; fortune-·telling remained a crime in England even after the repeal of the witchcraft acts in 1736.

Divination is, quite simply, the attempt to foretell the future or to discover secret knowledge by means of some instrument or agency. It has figured in religious practice since the dawn of written history and no doubt long before that. The very name reveals the profoundly awe-full implications of looking beyond the temporal limitations of the present, for to know the future is the prerogative of divinity and man does not lightly assume such rights. In antique eras, divination was looked upon not so much as coercive revelation, but the attempt to discover the will of the gods—not an enemy, but a part of religion. Its own degradation and the rise of Christianity contributed to its association with chicanery and devilry.

As the phenomenologist of archaic religion, G. Van der Leeuw, relates in his book *Religion in Essence and Manifestation*, divination was practiced (and still is in primitive cultures) not simply to discover what the future held, but to ascertain that what it held was congruent with the seeker's desires. Hence if augury produced unsatisfying results, repeated efforts were demanded until a suitable prediction was forthcoming. On this basis, Van der Leeuw suggests that the deeper religious purpose of divination, even as it was practiced by the ancient Hebrews, was to investigate the situation of proposed undertakings to assure that the time and place were propitious, that is, in accord with the will of God. In practice, a "portion" of the sacred totality, the cosmos, is consecrated (that is, set aside) and systematically interrogated in the belief that through the magical interconnections that underpin all manifest phenomena, the precise qualities of another particular place and time will be disclosed in their appropriate circumstances. Almost every conceivable natural and fabricated object has been used as a medium for divining the future in such a manner.

In Rome, *augurs* were perhaps the original priests; they became, at any rate, the chief members of the many classes of diviners in ancient Roman religion. The augur rendered events prosperous; our word "augment" is related to that function: "to increase." An archaic form of augury was watching the flights of birds to discover omens, signs portending future events. This early bird-watching ceremony was the duty of the "*auspex*," whose title gives us the words "auspicious" and "auspices." The *haruspex* divined propitious days for enterprises (wars, for instance) by examining the entrails of sacrificial animals and, apparently, also kept an eye on lightning and thunder.

Seeking for such signs of future events is not, of course, the only method of divining the gods' will. Dreams were (and are) universally considered to be harbingers of the future, the study of dream symbolism being called oneiromancy, from the Greek for "dream" and the suffix "*-manteia*," which meant "divination" and is commonly used for most varieties of that art. (Occasionally, a more pretentious "-ology" or "-osophy" is smuggled into the magical catalogue as in "phrenology"—divination by the shape of the skull—and "moleosophy"—the same by means of the size, shape, location, and color of moles and warts on the human body. Cheiromancy is not the same as cheirognomy, the former being divination by the lines in the palm, the latter a sort of character analysis based on the shape of the hand. *"Gnomon"* means "judge.") Divination was also practiced by conjuring the spirits of the dead—necromancy, and—the Grecian favorite—consulting oracles, who replied to questions about present or future concerns while in ecstasy. But by far the most common ancient and modern form of divination is the study of "signs" or omens, objects and events which magically portend the future.

Astromancy

Possibly the earliest of all forms of divination utilized the stars, which, as we have seen already, were believed to presage and even determine events on earth—more specially so remarkable occurrences as eclipses, comets, and novae. Attempting to foretell the future by astrological techniques is known as astromancy. Not all astrology is divination, nor was it in antiquity; even the common genethliacal variety was more a form of character analysis than an attempt to predict the future of the native. (Common newspaper astrology columns are largely astromantic, however, insofar as they pretend to give advice in advance regarding likely events determined by the position of the planets on that day.) It was possible for an adamant foe of divination such as Thomas Aquinas, who considered astromancy and other forms of the art to be sinfully idolatrous, to maintain all the same that, barring accidents, contingencies, and free will, all earthly events were influenced by the heavenly bodies. Edgar Cayce, though his cosmology was as thoroughly astrological as Aquinas's, likewise repudiated and condemned occult practices of prediction such as necromancy and ouija boards.

Other natural events, objects, and phenomena were employed to divine the future by archaic man—in fact, about everything conceivable has been so employed at one time or another. Among the more common we find clouds, water, fire, air, wind, salts, stones, eggs, soot, straw, the flight of birds, and the contents of animals' intestines. These have in turn given us the "sciences" of nephelomancy, hydromancy, pyromancy, aeromancy, austromancy, halomancy, lithomancy, ooscopy, spodomancy, sideromancy, as well as auspicy and haruspicy. The human body has added greatly to the diviner's hire, to wit: palmistry, in its twin forms of cheiromancy and cheirognomy, phrenology, physiognomy (divination by the shape and character of the face), moleosophy and various forms of temperamental and racial prognostications. Among human artifacts, numbers and letters have given us numerology and cryptography; cartomancy employs cards, such as the Tarot deck; scrying is another name for crystallomancy or gazing (for which a glass of water will do as well as a crystal ball and costs a lot less); sortilege refers to drawing lots, such as the tossing of coins or yarrow stalks (as in the *I Ching*), and includes the use of dice and dominoes; osteomancy comes from the study of bones; tasseography is the name for tea-leaf and coffee-ground reading; radiesthesia features divining rods and dowsing; ceromancy employs candle-drippings. There are more—pouring molten lead into water to see what pictures are formed, opening a book at random to find the answer to a problem—Virgil was a favorite author for this practice in the Middle Ages, the practice being called *sortes vergilianae*. Many otherwise orthodox Christians similarly employ the Bible for divination, a practice appropriately known as bibliomancy or stichomancy.

Human ingenuity has provided us with many more examples of divination, some of them rather comic to a modern reader (let future generations note), such as tiromancy or divination by cheese, and geloscopy, which is based on the sound of people's laughter. Walter and Litzka Gibson mention more than seventy-five other types of divination not listed here in their fascinating study of human superstition, *The Complete Illustrated Book of Psychic Sciences.*

Two kinds of divination demand at least a brief investigation—palmistry and the Tarot cards, the first because of its newly developing use by medical science and the police (which suggests a physical basis for the ancient superstition), and the second because the young have in particular become fascinated by the ancient deck, for reasons not the least of which is its very antiquity.

Palmistry

Man's opposable thumb distinguishes him from all other animals; on an observable, physiological basis, that splayed extremity, along with his upright position, has long fascinated man himself, particularly poets and scientists. Civilization is as much the work of man's hand, as the Psalmist tells us, as the frame of the universe is the handiwork of God.

In the dim pre-history of ancient India, where the art of palmistry seems to have developed, it was early noted that even the major lines in the human palm are individually peculiar. We now know that fingerprints (and toeprints) are as distinctive and unrepeatable as snowflakes, and that the pattern of blood vessels on the retina of the eye is as individually unique as a person's genetic pattern. But for the ancients, the first material proof of human individuality was found in the lines of the hand. Even astrology—perhaps the first attempt at psychology—could not assert so clearly the unicity of each human person, for people born at the same time in the same place, such as twins, triplets, or even neighbors, shared the same pattern of stars and planets. Man's individuality and, indeed, his destiny were read first in his own hand.

Why certain lines were associated with life, the emotions, intelligence, health, fame, and so forth is as obscure as is most of occult tradition: millenniums of observation have made it so, however, and tradition is its own justification. Much of the secondary lore of palmistry is derived from astrology, nonetheless, following the tendency of the magical arts to develop encompassing correspondences. Thus the parts of the palm between the lines—the bumps and depressions—are named for the planets: the Mount of Venus at the base of the thumb; that of Jupiter at the base of the index finger; Saturn, the middle; the sun or Apollo at the ring finger; and Mercury at the base of the little finger. The Mount of Mars is located below that of Mercury, and the Mount of the Moon is below that at the side of the palm near the wrist. Each of the Mounts has its own significance, similar to the astrological houses, indicating qualities of personality insofar as they are well-, over- or under-developed. The major *lines* of the hand are six: the lines of life, of the head, the heart, the line of Saturn or fate, the hepatic line or line of health, and the line of the sun or fortune. Minor lines include the girdle of Venus, Solomon's ring, lines of marriage and children, journeys, the wrist bracelets, the line of Mars, that of intuition, and the ominous *Via Lasciva* (fortunately rare). Each line, of course, has a particular significance depending on its length, depth, and variations, which can indicate everything from the length of life itself to how many children one will leave behind. Double lines, interrupted lines, "islands," wavy lines, chained lines, capillaried lines, and forked lines modify the significance of the major lines, and crosses, squares, triangles, stars, hatches or grill-marks, spots, and other small features made by intersections are very important for a correct interpretation. Of course, variations and combinations are as endless as the genetic pattern of the race are diverse (See diagram, page 154.)

Cheirognomy, the "science" of the hand itself, deals with the shape, size, and quality of the whole hand, as well as with the length of the fingers, their phalanges, the angle between thumb and index finger, between the fingers themselves, the relative knottiness of the knuckles, the smoothness or roughness of the skin, and so forth, all of which (and more) are held to indicate character and personality. Count Louis Hamon's book *Cheiro's Complete Palmistry,* available in paperback, is a comprehensive text for anyone who might wish to devote further time to the study of palmistry.

What is more remarkable about palmistry (than its survival) is its increasing use among doctors and the law's enforcers. Fingerprinting is by now, of course, a common practice of both agencies. Recently, the *Journal* of the American Medical Association has featured articles which treat of studying the hands of new-born infants for signs of cryptic birth defects. Called dermato-glyphics (as occult a sound as ever uttered), this new science is based on the fact that some infants who will only later manifest behavioral symptoms of retardation have characteristic lines in their handprints at birth. Recognizing these, doctors can begin early treatment to forestall further damage or even provide a cure.

Chromosomal damage can also be detected in the skin of babies whose mothers have been exposed to measles. Certain abnormalities in the lines of both hands and feet can reveal pre-natal injury. The scientific basis for this kind of correlation between manifest physical traits and genetic or even physiological dysfunction is the "law" of polyploidy-polygeny, which means that each gene which a person inherits affects *all* characteristics at least in a secondary way, and that *each* characteristic is influenced by the entire genetic panoply. Science has long known that each gene has a determinate effect on a single characteristic, but we are only beginning to appreciate the effects of the interplay between all the genes and all the characteristics that make a person his unique self. This is but one instance of the direction of modern science and medicine away from departmentalization towards a holistic understanding of man, his body, and his mind.

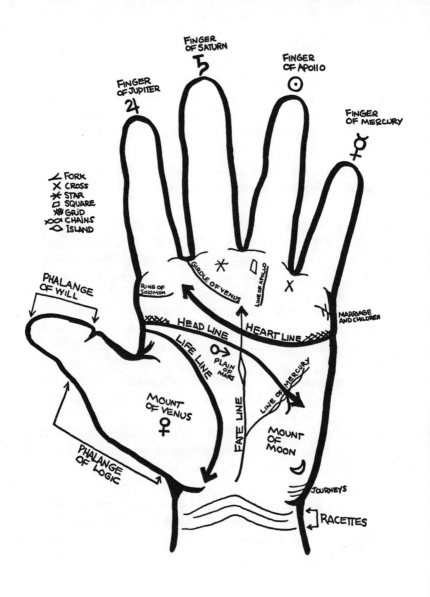

FINGER
OF SATURN

FINGER
OF APOLLO

FINGER
OF JUPITER

FINGER
OF MERCURY

⅃ FORK
✕ CROSS
✳ STAR
▢ SQUARE
✻ GRID
⋈ CHAINS
◇ ISLAND

PHALANGE
OF WILL

GIRDLE OF VENUS

RING OF
SOLOMON

LINE OF APOLLO

MARRIAGE
AND CHILDREN

HEAD LINE

HEART LINE

LIFE LINE

PLAIN
OF
MARS

LINE OF MERCURY

FATE LINE

MOUNT
OF VENUS
♀

MOUNT
OF
MOON

PHALANGE
OF LOGIC

JOURNEYS

RACETTES

154

Consequently, it is not too surprising that the age-old arts of palmistry, phrenology, physiognomy, and graphology (character analysis by a study of handwriting, which has been in use by psychologists for some time) should have survived the rigors of the scientific revolution that began in the seventeenth century. Like astrology, such enterprises have sufficient basis in the experience of mankind to resist hasty denunciation. Whether moleosophy will prove of value remains to be seen, but already skin disorders are being investigated as indications of a tendency to cancer and other diseases. The unity of the mind and body, long a cherished tenet of occultism, has certainly been verified by the validation of psychosomatic medicine.

Deciphering character and personal history from physical traits is, on the other hand, a tenuous extrapolation of medical science, however responsible we are for our faces, as Camus maintained. To extend the facts to cover predicting the future is more tenuous yet. What we shall be physiologically is unmistakably imprinted in our genotypes and read in our fingerprints. How we are faring may be deciphered there as well. But what we make of our lives, interacting with other people and events, is something of quite another order.

The Tarot

As we might expect by now, the origin of the Tarot deck is obscure. A Parisian museum boasts the oldest deck in captivity, that made for mad King Charles VI in 1392. According to conflicting legends, the cards were designed as a sort of philosophical shorthand by the Magi of Fez in the thirteenth century after the destruction of Alexandria. Paul Christian maintains that the arcane symbolism derives from the pictures lining the secret hall that connected the sphinx to the Great Pyramid as recorded by Iamblichus. Other students assert that the cards came from India by way of Persia, along with palmistry.

Whatever their origin, the seventy-eight cards are a chief magical instrument and the most popular form of contemporary (and possibly traditional) divinatory objects. They are rife with correspondences to cabalistic lore, alchemy, numerology, astrology, and other branches of the magical tree. The name *Tarot* is perhaps an anagram for the Latin *"rota"* ("wheel"), although it has been long associated with the Torah, and there are other explanations which are no more (or less) convincing.

The deck is divided into two parts—the fifty-six cards of the Minor Arcana, the prototype of our familiar playing cards, and twenty-two cards of the Major Arcana, originally unnumbered. *Hair*'s "Magician" and "The Lovers" derive from this part of the Tarot. Occultists have arranged these cards in a fairly systematic fashion, "rectifying" them according to their own magical theories, a practice especially true of Eliphas Levi, A. E. Waite, and Aleister Crowley. The common pattern of the traditional deck (there are "modern" versions as well) is as follows: 0. The Fool; 1. The Magician (or Juggler); 2. The High-Priestess; 3. The Empress; 4. The Emperor; 5. The Hierophant (Pope); 6. The Lovers; 7. The Chariot; 8. Strength (sometimes Justice is placed here); 9. The Hermit; 10. The Wheel of Fortune; 11. Justice (or Strength); 12. The Hanged Man; 13. Death; 14. Temperance; 15. The Devil; 16. The Tower; 17. The Star; 18. The Moon; 19. The Sun; 20. Judgment; 21. The World.

The Minor Arcana is divided into four suits: Wands (Staves), Cups, Swords, and Pentacles (Coins). In late medieval France, these were transformed into our more familiar but cognate clubs, hearts, spades, and diamonds. There are fourteen cards in each suit, ten cards numbered from ace to ten, and four "court cards"—page, knight, queen, and king. (Interestingly enough, the knights, which were to figure so ominously in the note left by the slayer of the Ohta family, were eliminated from the deck as it was reduced to the customary use it now has in gaming; the "Jack" or "knave" is the older "page.")

The court cards have a further significance than the obvious one; the inquirer seeking his fortune is represented by one of them, which is chosen according to his (her) resemblance. A man in his maturity will be represented by a king, a young man by a knight, all women by a queen. A young man, for instance, with black hair and dark eyes corresponds to the knight of swords; a blond, blue-eyed young woman would be the queen of wands. The court cards can also symbolize the human person in its "parts"—the body by the page, the ego or mind by the knight, the soul by the queen, and the spirit by the king. Specific persons can also be represented by court cards as they are turned up during the reading.

Various methods of reading the cards have been devised over the centuries, the most famous being that based on the cabalistic "tree of life" and the "Celtic" method (both explained in Eden Gray's *The Tarot Revealed*). The simplest method is just to cut the deck. In the more elaborate methods, the pattern of the cards—whether they are reversed or upright, which cards appear next to each other, whether repeated readings turn up the same card and so forth—is the key to understanding their message. Of course, it is first necessary for the reader to have a complete mastery of the occult symbolism packed into each card, perhaps the reason why carnival fortune-tellers and ordinary gypsies prefer the standard playing card deck, which has been simplified to mere numbers and symbols, thus permitting a wide range of individual interpretations.

Most people have one question foremost in their minds when confronted by the Tarot-wielding adept: does it work? Apparently so—as much as any form of divination does or, for that matter, psychotherapy. Everything depends on the investment of the inquirer and what he contributes actively to the revelatory process. One explanation for the "magic" of the cards, which touches on ESP, is that since the inquirer must shuffle or at least cut the deck, he subconsciously arranges the cards in a certain order. To dismiss such an idea as merest nonsense is itself a form of prejudice today, as researchers the world over delve into the "hidden" powers of the mind. But it must be admitted that no one has yet proved or even substantiated such a hypothetical explanation. Nevertheless, the continuing success of the cards—at least their popularity—testifies to the value they possess for those who consult them, whether in boardwalk booth or the hippie dens of the occult revolution.

Divination: How It Works

While it is not my intention to prove or disprove anything about the magical practices in the occult revolution, it is possibly wise to point out that the success of predictions can be ascribed in many cases to a psychological "catch" which has been called the "halo effect." One swallow does not make a summer (or an alcoholic), but a single, accurate statement—no matter how coincidental—made by a diviner, whether the most amateur Tarot enthusiast or the most unconscionable journalist-astrologer, seems to be sufficient to convince the credulous that there is, indeed, "truth" in it (whatever "it" happens to be). We believe what we want to believe, and discount what does not fit in with our preconceptions, a very subtle form of auto-suggestion. In other words, when our situation inclines us to favor reliance on a proposed "authority," correct predictions reinforce our positive attitude, while mistakes are ignored.

Another "catch" that figures throughout the history of magic and occultism, especially with regard to divination, is the "self-fulfilling prophecy." Once we accept the authority of the "prophet," we are likely to interpret events to fit the prophecy or even act in accordance with the prediction whether or not we do so consciously. Robert K. Merton, the great sociological theorist, developed a comprehensive account of this mechanism of human belief. In effect, we prove what we first accepted as inevitable.

Divination, the least dramatic of the magical arts and sciences, can be the most captivating by dint of its subtle "catches." In several personal experiences. I have witnessed sober, intelligent (as well as devout) people become more and more entranced by the "accuracy" of ouija boards or astrology columns even while professing disbelief. I have also met high school students who are as "hooked" on Tarot cards as others are on drugs—whether or not these drugs are themselves addictive. The harm lies in the mental and spiritual environment of the credulous, not so much in the quality of the "magic."

Herein lies the bane as well as the promise of much of the occult revolution. The spreading bankruptcy of social and moral values, exaggerated but nonetheless really perceived by the young dissenters who have dropped out of the "system," creates a need for an alternative code of values, an "alternative authority," if you will. For many of the young, technology, affluence, and even the organized churches have abdicated their authority by "selling out" to a corrupt establishment—what the early Christians designated "the world." And they quickly found the alternative authorities which they had been bred to need: Eastern mysticism, drugs, radical protest movements, and occultism. Each of these has its good as well as harmful aspects, occultism no less than the others. For the occult revolution is a spiritual awakening, threatened to be sure by the temptation to settle for cheap magical tricks, but also pregnant with possibilities for opening new vistas of mental and spiritual progress—a deeper understanding of human potential and perhaps a new development in our awareness of the less obvious mechanics of the mysterious universe which is our home.

9.

The Dawn of Mind

Do events cast their shadows ahead of themselves? Are events both the cause and the effect of our perception of them? Can our dreams and intimations determine the shape of future events?

The relationship between temporal events and our awareness of them in space and time is an age-old problem for the human mind, calling into question our understanding of the very nature of reality and existence. Recent investigations into relativity physics, indeterminacy, time-bending, and so on have hardly diminished interest in the ancient puzzle, but rather have reinforced it from "the other side." We are, as a race, more convinced than ever that things may not be what they seem.

Having become the object of serious attention by scientists, engineers, and technologists, including those of the United States Army and NASA, many formerly occult phenomena such as clairvoyance and telepathy, although not of obvious relevance to the occult revolution, are stimulating far-ranging discussions and are well known to the young. Hence we shall conclude our tour of the major areas of our subject with a somewhat cursory investigation of two modern mystics, Edgar Cayce and Jeane Dixon, which will warrant a discursus into the topics of prophecy, reincarnation, ESP and spiritualism, hypnosis, and the promise of a new understanding of mind from the emerging synthesis of science and mysticism.

The Sleeping Prophet

On Tuesday, February 9, 1970, following a lunar eclipse and during the full moon, Southern California was shaken awake by a severe earthquake which left scores of people dead and injured. Seismic events are not rare even in California, but far less fear and panic accompany much worse quakes in South America and Turkey, countries which have been devastated by recent tremors, than that which followed this shock and its after-shocks. Hundreds of people, children as well as adults, enlisted in group therapy sessions to allay their anxiety, and once again, people began to think about one of America's strangest figures—the "sleeping prophet" of Virginia Beach, Virginia—Edgar Cayce.

Before his death in 1945, Cayce predicted that by the turn of the century, California would break apart and slide under the waves of the Pacific ocean. He also said that the eastern sea-coast of the United States would be disrupted and flooded in a similar fashion, but since earthquakes are uncommon east of the Rockies, not too many easterners are anxious about their lives and property. California, on the other hand, the homeland of offbeat religions and self-appointed mystics and messiahs, seems to have taken the Cayce prophecies with less than a grain of salt. The eschatological feeling that was spawned there in the recent past has been exported to the cities and communes where Haight-Ashbury is remembered as fondly as Camelot, and among the members of the burgeoning counter culture, the name of Edgar Cayce is mentioned with respect. His popularity has been enhanced by his organic food preferences, his teachings about reincarnation and karma, his version of Atlantis, and Christian eclecticism.

Edgar Cayce's life resembles that of other mystics and seers in some respects, such as the discovery of his powers at an early age, his struggles, his refusal to accept monetary compensation for readings, and his catastrophic predictions. But he also differs

161

in many other ways, especially in his odd syncretism of orthodox and exotic religious themes, his teachings about reincarnation, astrology, food, and also Atlantis. Most strange of all, perhaps, was his method of giving readings. Oracles from ancient Greece spoke in a delirium produced by inhaling fumes, and Mexican Indians rely on the peyote bud; whole societies go into religious trances simultaneously, and mediums are often known to "sleep" as the "spirits" speak through them. But Cayce, while he resembles many of these classical "prophets," remains strikingly singular. While in a self-induced trance, he would speak not of discarnate spirits in some other plane, but of living human beings in his presence or thousands of miles distant. When he more or less stumbled into reincarnation while in trance, he found that he had the ability to tell of others' past lives rather than the usual form of hypnotic seance where the subject is "regressed" back to his own previous incarnations. His psychometric ability to diagnose illnesses was incredibly accurate; few errors have ever been found.

He was born in rural Kentucky in 1877 and died at Virginia Beach, Virginia, on January 3, 1945, exhausted by the rigors of a life selflessly dedicated to helping others—his last years were spent giving daily readings for servicemen and their families, far beyond the number his body could tolerate, thus hastening his death.

As a boy, Cayce showed signs of possessing abnormal "powers." When he was about seven, he experienced a religious vision in which he learned that his prayers to be able to help mankind would be answered. Thereafter, clairvoyance, especially the ability to diagnose illnesses at a distance, began to manifest itself—first on his own behalf, when he advised his parents how to treat a baseball injury. Although not a denominationalist, Cayce's religious background was Presbyterian, and he remained a devout Christian throughout his life, reading the entire Bible from cover to cover every year. His psychic abilities were recognized as a gift of God by the famout evangelistic preacher Dwight Moody, whose counsel the young Cayce had sought when considering entering the ministry.

Afflicted with a throat disorder a few years later, Cayce was treated by an itinerant hypnotist at his own request after all orthodox methods had failed to cure him. This event had a profound effect on his career, for while in trance, he again diagnosed his own illness and effected a cure by hypnotic suggestion. Later, he prescribed a cure for the hypnotist himself and, after serious reflection, began giving readings for others. His reputation spread quickly—as a prophet and as a freak.

Cayce married Gertrude Evens at this time and she became his life-long support, encouraging him to continue his ministry against sometimes hopeless obstacles. Edgar sought work as a photographer and devoted himself to teaching Sunday school. But his gift effectively prevented him from other work than healing and teaching, which he eventually recognized was the answer to his youthful prayers.

Cayce's career as a healer was not an easy life; he was ridiculed by neighbors and lampooned by the press. He was actually prosecuted by police and medical authorities, although he was always acquitted of the charges. He later attempted to establish a college and a hospital, but both went bankrupt in 1931. Through the years, however, he was supported by his wife and Gladys Davis, his secretary, who became a member of the Cayce household and remained his close associate until his death. At Virginia Beach, Gladys, now Mrs. Gladys Davis Turner, still supervises the editing and cross-indexing of the 50,000 pages of testimony transcribed by her from Edgar's two daily readings.

Under the guidance of Edgar's son, Hugh Lynn Cayce, the Association for Research and Enlightenment (ARE) continues the work of America's leading mystic, especially by the promotion of books. At least four biographies of Cayce have been written, and the latest, Jess Stern's *Edgar Cayce—The Sleeping*

Prophet, attained the rank of a bestseller. There are, in addition, a dozen editions compiled from readings which include topics such as astrology, diet, reincarnation, and a fantastic interpretation of biblical history edited by Jeffrey Furst, *Edgar Cayce's Story of Jesus.*

From an empirical standpoint, the most amazing of Cayce's talents was that of diagnosis at a distance, which first gained him the attention of the press and the medical profession. Despite a few undisputed cases of failure, which were not so much the result of an erroneous diagnosis as instances of a failure to follow the mystic's recommendations or a simple lack of time needed for a cure, Cayce's record of healing—even incurable diseases—is remarkable in every respect. In many instances, probably most, he did not know or ever see his patients, nor did he pray for them or attempt to influence their physical condition in any way other than prescriptions regarding diet, exercises (many of which were yoga-like), and occasionally treatment by ultraviolet radiation. He had little use for surgery. His remedies were always particular, and even a cross-comparison (such as can be found in *Edgar Cayce Speaks*) fails to produce nostrums that can be followed by all and sundry.

On August 10, 1923, Cayce was giving a reading for Arthur Lammers, a student of Eastern mysticism, when he unwittingly discovered the most controversial element of his "doctrine." Lammers had questioned the sleeping Cayce concerning reincarnation, and the devout, Bible-bred Protestant Sunday-school teacher obliged him with a series of unmistakably affirmative statements. On awakening, Cayce was horrified and all but repudiated the whole business. Pressed by Lammers, Cayce reread the entire Bible and concluded that there was no essential contradiction between biblical faith and reincarnationism, a view hardly shared by most Protestants, needless to add, especially those of a conservative and fundamentalist bent. Until his death, however, Cayce gave "life readings" for people of all faiths, dealing with events that antedate all recorded history. Thus he discovered Atlantis.

Over the years from 1923 to his death in 1945, Edgar Cayce developed the only original version of the story of Atlantis other than Plato's accounts in the *Timaeus* and the *Critias*. (For an excellent summary of recent non-mystical thought on the subject of Atlantis, one can profitably consult Willy Ley's *Another Look at Atlantis*.) As a seventh-grade graduate, Cayce cannot be suspected of deriving his teaching from reading Plato (although, contrary to some opinions, Cayce was a literate and highly intelligent man). And not only did Cayce describe a huge continent called Atlantis which existed in the Atlantic Ocean between 10,000,000 B.C. and 10,000 B.C., when it was inundated, but he spoke of another lost continent in the Pacific, Lemuria, which met a similar fate. Both will rise again, he predicted, before the turn of the present century.

Other catastrophic events that Cayce predicted for the world beginning in 1958 and lasting until 1998 have had their effect on contemporary consciousness, as is evident in the Californian apocalyptic anxiety. Student of "secular" prophecy can have a holiday correlating Cayce's time-table with prophecies by Nostradamus, St. Malachy, and other seers, not the least of whom is still alive and well in Washington, D.C.—Jeane Dixon, whose fame is, if anything, greater than Cayce's and the others' combined.

An American Prophetess

Perhaps because of her politically sensitive location, Washington's seeress, Jeane Dixon, has become an American legend, a contemporary avatar of Clytemnestra. Long noted for her often (but not always) accurate predictions, Mrs. Dixon gained international attention when it was learned that she had foreseen the assassination of John Kennedy and had attempted to warn him against that fatal trip to Dallas. She also predicted the assassinations of Martin Luther King and Bobby Kennedy. Among her other predictions, made well in advance of their realization, were the deaths of Carole Lombard, Roosevelt, Gandhi, Marilyn Monroe, Nehru, Dag Hammarskjold, Churchill, and John Foster Dulles; the fall of China (three years in advance), the partition of India, Truman's and Eisenhower's elections, as well as Nixon's; the launching of the first Sputnik; the Alaskan earthquake of 1964 (four weeks in advance); the summoning of the Second Vatican Council a year before it happened; and many more lesser events and catastrophes.

Not all of Mrs. Dixon's prophecies are dire, but often they turn about the death of some renowned person or a serious calamity, much as have the traditional prophecies of all nations and times. Important for a proper evaluation, but proving little, are Mrs. Dixon's "false" prophecies: that Lyndon Johnson would gain the Democratic candidacy in 1968 (Humphrey did); her denial up to a day before the Onassis wedding that Jacqueline Kennedy would remarry; that the "China problem" would be solved in 1953; that Russia would invade Iran in 1953 and Palestine in 1957; that World War III would begin in 1958; that Communist China would gain entry to the United Nations in 1959; that the Vietnamese war would end by 1966; that Russia would be first to land a man on the moon; and other instances. Much of these "failures" has been made by Mrs. Dixon's critics, particularly in Bjornstad's *Twentieth Century Prophecy*. Factually, we are left with both correct and incorrect predictions, the interpretation of which depends a good deal on what one wishes to prove. To the best of my knowledge, Mrs. Dixon has never claimed infallibility, and her "true" (that is, fulfilled) prophecies are as amazing as her mistakes are embarrassing.

Jeane Pinckert Dixon was born in 1918 of German emigrant parents who at that time lived in Medford, Wisconsin. Her father grew fairly wealthy and the family retired to Santa Rosa, California, where they established ties with the famous Luther Burbank. When Jeane was eight years old, a gypsy fortune-teller was discovered encamped on the Burbank estate, and Jeane's mother, a devout Catholic but possessed of many old-world beliefs, took the child to the woman for a reading. The gypsy was astonished by the lines in the tiny palms, and announced that Jeane would become a famous seeress, having the "gift of prophecy." Thereupon the woman presented Jeane with a crystal ball in which the child could see "pictures." Later, a Hindu mystic told Jeane's mother that the startling lines in the girl's palms appeared in such patterns about once in every thousand years and confirmed the gypsy's prediction of her coming greatness.

For several years, Jeane's life was that of an ordinary California girl in the halcyon days before Hollywood became the true capital and spiritual center of the West. Occasionally, however, she would announce to her startled family that certain events were about to occur and her predictions were often fulfilled exactly. Once she advised a despondent actress, Marie Dressler, against giving up her career, promising her a successful future, which was certainly no mistake.

Marrying James Dixon, an automobile dealer, Jeane Pinckert found herself moving first to Detroit, then to Washington, as World War II burst on the country. Her husband had volunteered to handle property acquisitions for the War Department for a dollar-a-year salary. Jeane likewise involved herself in social service and charitable programs, but her psychic abilities earned her even greater attention. She began giving readings to servicemen and later to politicians. She once told Harry Truman that he would become President by "an act of God."

So famous has she become that Jeane was eventually summoned to the White House, not once but twice, during the last year of Roosevelt's life. Among other predictions, Jeane told the President that he would die within six months.

Jeane Dixon's career continued to flourish in Washington, where she and her family still live. Her story and predictions can be read in detail in Ruth Montgomery's *A Gift of Prophecy,* and her own *My Life and Prophecies.*

Although America abounds with seers and prophets, Jeane Dixon shares with Edgar Cayce the major acclaim of the new occultists (and many others), perhaps not least because of her startling announcements relative to the "Child of the East," a boy born on February 5, 1962, the day of the great Aquarian conjunction. On that day, Jeane had a vision which was puzzling and unnerving. Eventually, she interpreted it as meaning that a child had been born in the Near East who would one day revolutionize the religions and governments of the world. He will reach the pinnacle of his power in 1999, when a terrible holocaust will shock the world's peoples into a true renewal. For the child, she finally decided, is not a new messiah, but the anti-Christ who will lead most of humanity away from God's chosen path. The child's purpose is, Jeane claims, satanic, but his life will initially parallel that of Jesus—even to his sudden appearance on the world scene when he is about thirty.

Eventually the triumphs of this satanic emissary will be swallowed up by Christ's victory, but only after a terrible struggle. How much of this interpretation is taken from Christian tradition is hard to determine, but the similarity to Revelations is, of course, evident. And it is this, plus the astrological coincidence of the date of February 5, 1962, the Caycean, Nostradamus-like 1999, and the cataclysmic predictions for that era which stand Jeane Dixon in the ranks of many other seers who stir the eschatological embers providing a good deal of the heat in the occult revolution.

Objectionable in Whole and Part?

Many religious writers have expressed concern at the spreading influence of the teachings of Cayce and Jeane Dixon, for although both are avowedly Christian, both are likewise decidedly heterodox. Edgar Cayce's pronouncements on Atlantis, astrology, reincarnation, and the life of Christ, together with Jeane Dixon's employment of occult paraphernalia, including crystal balls, finger-touching, palm-reading, cards, and astrology have drawn in particular the fire of orthodox proponents of traditional Christianity. Regrettably, in the heat of debate, what is most apparent is that what is being offered in lieu of certain personal interpretations of Christianity is another, more traditional but equally personal interpretation. Scriptural quotations are used as ammunition on both sides, proving of little damage to either. James Bjornstad's *Twentieth Century Prophecy* is a noteworthy example of argument which proceeds from prejudice to presupposition via a highly selective and narrowly sectarian interpretation of Scripture.

Bjornstad's angry attack on Cayce and Dixon raises some important questions for Christians, however, especially those regarding natural prophetic charism, the possibility of false or mistaken predictions and the problem of interpretation. Unfortunately, little consensus can be appealed to even with regard to true, God-given prophecies, for scholars and exegetes recognize the delicacy of affirmations and denials relative to what is meant by disputed passages of scripture.

We wonder, then, is there true prophecy outside of the line of biblical prophets? Could their prophecies have been wrong? Is prophecy an abiding gift or did it cease with the apostles? This last question is of some interest to many pentecostally inclined Christians today, even though they often seem exclusively attuned to glossolalia—the gift of tongues, which Paul rated rather below that of prophecy (1, Cor. 14).

169

Prophets and Prophecy

Nearly every major Catholic, Protestant, and Jewish theologian has at one time or another essayed into the difficult area of prophetic inspiration and activity: Paul, Augustine, and Aquinas, of course, and more "recently," Wellhausen, Kittel, Gunkel, and Mowinkel; Rowley, Buber, and even Max Weber; Robinson, Napier, and Porteous; Ronald Knox, Rahner, and Benoit; Schillebeeckx and Kung; Barth and Tillich and Bultmann.

Summarily, the traditional Catholic view was perhaps first enunciated by Thomas Aquinas, who defined prophecy as a kind of knowledge supernaturally given to man which exceeds what he could know by his own efforts and which is offered for the good of the community. True prophetic knowledge is given only by God, and is therefore inevitably true, although the prophet can sometimes confuse what comes to him from God and what is of his own "spirit." Nevertheless, prophecy as foreknowledge of the future is possibly a natural endowment insofar as by natural disposition of the intellect and imagination a man might be able to discover the shape of coming events by understanding present causes of future effects. True, God-given prophecy, however, needs no previous disposition on the part of the recipient, not even a good moral life. Prophecy, Aquinas held, can even come through demonic agencies and yet be true, although divine revelations can never be false. Cases of "error," such as Jonah's prophecy against Ninevah and Jesus' assertion that not a brick would be left on a brick of the Temple wall (one whole wall is still standing), are conditional prophecies, threats that would be carried out if people did not repent, and so forth.

Karl Rahner, attempting to present a more contemporary Catholic view of prophecy, suggests that under that heading could be listed five types: the magical, such as soothsaying; parapsychological; an anticipation of the future by the study of trends in history, and so on; fabricated prophecies (invented after the fact); and genuine supernatural revelations from God.

Protestant theologians tend to view prophecy less as an intellectual charism than a mode of life; A. C. Porteous in his *Prophetic Voices in Contemporary Theology* lists several criteria by which a prophet may be known: he enunciates a fresh articulation of the word of God, conforming to the essential and traditional aspects of Revelation; he challenges contemporary idolatries; he claims to speak for God in special historical moments of crisis; and he stirs up resentment and resistance from those to whom his message is directed—those who defend the status quo in matters of cult and creed.

A conservative spokesman such as Bjornstad seems to acknowledge only two major sources of prophecy: God and demons, although he does not seem to rule out the possibility of some kind of natural gift for predicting the future. Neither he nor anyone else—including Jeane Dixon and Edgar Cayce—would claim that these American prophets were divinely inspired as were Elijah and Isaiah. The real question centers on whether "natural" prophecy or demonic prophecy is at work, or whether God is using them as he once used the prophet of Baal, Balaam (Num. 22, 5). Both Cayce and Jeane Dixon represent devout, God-loving, and religious examples of service to mankind, which are significant "fruits" (cf. Mt. 7, 20), at any rate.

In brief, most contemporary theologians agree that prophecy as such did not die out with the closing of the apostolic age, but continues both in and outside the Church, as God-directed inspiration and action. "True" prophets can sometimes make mistakes, but on their own; "false" prophets can predict accurately, whether by God's working through their natural or special abilities. Demonic agents may also work "prophetically," outside any incidence of ESP or natural acuity of historical analysis, which brings up the knotty problem of contemporary disbelief in demons. Let us say for now that it is conceivable that extra-human forces—whether understood as social powers or malevolent spirits—can influence someone in such wise that he becomes the unwitting agent of destructive energies—a Manson or a Goebbels.

In the life of the Church, prophecy is a variable phenomenon; it has been given for the sake of the people, not the prophet, and does not depend on human power or frailty for its warrant and worth. We shall thus reserve judgment on the prophetic character of Edgar Cayce and Jeane Dixon from a theological point of view howsoever much their unorthodoxy might frighten us. Had either of them maintained that they were God's prophets to the modern world, there might be reason for objection. Both seers claim to have received their gifts from God, but that is a rather different matter from speaking for God. And from the perspective of the occult revolution, the nature of their gifts is of more concern than how they got them, for both manifest abilities associated with what is now called ESP—extrasensory perception, which is all the more fascinating because of the vague religious feeling that even the mention of such things elicits in most of us.

The categories of precognition, retrocognition, clairvoyance, and object-reading can account for the gifts of Edgar Cayce and Jeane Dixon without recourse to a "supernatural" explanation, if we abide by the principle of parsimony, which means that when we can choose between hypotheses, we should incline towards the simpler. For many of us, entering the domain of the "paranormal" or "psychic" is not necessarily easier than thinking in terms of angels and devils, but it is more honest. But if we thus plan to avoid the pitfalls of theological investigation, what will account for the starting talents of persons such as Cayce, Jeane Dixon, Peter Hurkos, Ted Serios, Arthur Ford, and the hundreds of other mediums, seers, and mystics whose experiences seem so other-worldly? Research scientists are beginning to explore the unknown zones of the human mind (and the brain) to answer that query, and they are learning some very interesting things about our experience of the world.

The Science of Mind

Living as we do in the aftermath of the Enlightenment, it may not seem surprising that the mandarins of science have steadfastly refused up to now to acknowledge so much as the possible existence of such things as clairvoyance and telepathy, and the very mention of the word "ghost" could invite gales of laughter or scorn. Perhaps such a seemingly irrational prejudice (amply testified to in the story of Joseph Banks Rhine and the Duke University experiments) is partly responsible for the favor and enthusiasm with which the anti-technocratic occult revolutionaries have adopted ouija boards, Tarot cards, and the armor of belief in the supernatural. The world of the occult may be the Last Sanctuary.

Scientific intolerance may also be responsible for the very continuation of the occult tradition in its gloomiest aspects, as the disfavor with which the medical and legal professions, as well as the scientific community, regarded hypnotism for many years, permitting it to remain a stage magician's trick rather than enter its proper domain in hospitals and laboratories as it has in Europe, where theatrical hypnotism is illegal. Not long ago, however, Dr. G. H. Estabrooks could write, "There is not a reputable psychologist in the United States who would dare write an article questioning the existence of hypnotism and certain phenomena in hypnotism. His reputation would be ruined if he did. But in the case of spiritism, and psychic research, the exact opposite is true."[1] Dr. Estabrooks maintains that many allegedly occult phenomena, particularly those involving mediums, trances, automatic writing, scrying, levitation, and the like, are actually

[1] *Hypnotism,* New York, 1957, page 76.

173

hypnotic in origin, but the steadfast refusal to consider experimenting with such events and states has prevented a scientific evaluation of ESP—until recently, that is.

Within the past five years, there has been a subtle but constant transformation of scientific attitude towards paranormal experiences. Several universities have quietly established departments for parapsychological research since Dr. Rhine left Duke in 1965 after a conflict with the administration. In 1967, Dr. J. G. Pratt, formerly of the University of Virginia, and Dr. Ian Stevenson, also of Virginia, tested the psychic abilities of Ted Serios, a Chicago bellhop, gaining international attention. Dr. Pratt is now the treasurer of the American Parapsychological Association and presides over the Psychical Research Foundation. Stevenson is Alumni Professor of Psychiatry at the University of Virginia, whose interest in reincarnation has been featured in recent books and magazines.

American scientists are somewhat behind their British counterparts in the area of parapsychological research. The British Society for Psychical Research was established by Edmund Gurney and Frederick Myers in 1882, and is a highly respectable association. The guiding spirit of the early SPR was Professor Henry Sidgwick of Cambridge, and among the notable scholars who gathered about the trio of researchers were Earl Balfour, Henri Bergson, Hans Driesch, and the Americans William James and William McDougall. The American Society for Psychic Research was founded in 1888, and the present President of that group is Dr. Gardner Murphy of the Menninger Foundation. Many superb scientists have belonged to both groups, and other nations have similar organizations, most of which have been publishing their findings for decades. But professional associations of scientists, particularly psychologists, who themselves had many a prejudice to overcome before they were accepted into the academic community, have been extremely reticent to acknowledge the validity of even research techniques among the parapsychologists, whose methodology has often been exquisitely precise and controlled. Fortunately, the perseverance of the pioneering founders of the new discipline was greater than the prejudice of their critics. (Two excellent source books on early psychical research are R. C. Johnson's *Psychical Research* and Professor C. E. M. Hansel's *ESP: A Scientific Evaluation*.)

In general, psychic researches recognize several varieties of extrasensory experience or parapsychological phenomena: clairvoyance, clairaudience, and telepathy, which involve seeing, hearing, or "knowing" things at a distance; precognition and retrocognition, which are knowledge of events from the future or past (precognition coming close to what we referred to as "natural prophecy"); object reading, by which a subject can relate information about a person (generally) on the basis of some object they have owned or touched; psychokinesis and levitation, the ability to influence material objects (including the body) by thought; materialization, "ectoplasmic" projections; apparitions and hauntings, including poltergeist phenomena; and various less dramatic talents, events, and so forth: glossolalia and xenoglossy—the ability to speak ecstatically or in a foreign tongue, mediumistic talents, automatic writing, and so on.

Many of these phenomena are considered by psychical researchers to be produced by individual persons with extraordinary mental "powers." These "powers" may be forms of behavior otherwise considered pathological; for instance, a medium who speaks with the voice of a "spirit guide" manifests many of the same patterns of behavior as do patients suffering from multiple-personality—a rare form of schizophrenia which was portrayed in the excellent film *The Three Faces of Eve*. The medium, however, is not psychotic. In fact, most mediums are very ordinary people.

Dr. Estabrooks suggests that many of the abilities of psychics can be explained by auto-suggestion, and many of their feats can also be attributed to subtle hypnotic powers which they perhaps unwittingly exercise over their clients. Yoga trances are similar to hypnotic states, and such conditions also produce uncanny results in both the subject and their environment.

Disputes continue, experiments go on, and the practitioners of occultism attend to their business more or less attentive to what happens in the halls of academies. For centuries, literally, the same kind of claims, the same type of subjects were examined and described by societies such as the old Freemasons, the Rosicrucians, the Theosophical Society founded by the mysterious Madame Blavatsky, the Order of the Golden Dawn, and others. That the Center for Studies in Democratic Institutions is now interested in these matters is hardly impressive to wizards and magicians, nor is it to the religious devotees of Mary Baker Eddy or those who follow scientology. After all, they were there first.

From a religious viewpoint, and that means in terms of the occult revolution as well, the emergence of a scientific interest in ESP is of secondary importance to its value in reaffirming the power of the human mind. Young witches may never have heard of the American Society for Psychical Research, but they are highly conscious of the promise of ESP and cultivate it. Hallucinogenic experiences have created more interest in mental states than have the researches of J. B. Rhine, at least among the counter-cultural youth. Seances, table-turning, spiritualism, and precognition are also powerful hints that supernaturalism is far from absent in contemporary society, as Peter Berger began to suspect in *A Rumor of Angels,* although in a rather less "traditional" manner. The belief in a larger world than that revealed by science and one less empty than that proposed by radical theologians has great attractiveness to the dissenters in modern society who are eager for signs of a truer authority than political or scientific expertise. Perhaps it is the only refuge beyond technology.

A Word About Reincarnation

Christians have balked more at the strange belief in multiple existence on earth than on any other element on modern occultism, with the possible exception of satanism. Yet among mankind's religious and ethical beliefs, few are as persistent as reincarnationism; it is found in Plato and the writings of Eastern mystics, particularly in Hinduism and Buddhism, but it also enjoyed a brief period of Christian enthusiasm among the Origenists of the third and fourth century. Today, Margaret Mead once said, referring to a religious census, one out of seven Englishmen still believes in it. Even in the Gospels, we read that many of Jesus' contemporaries considered him a reincarnation of Elijah and Herod thought that he might be John the Baptist come back from the dead. Paul's assertion that Jesus was "the second Adam" has been interpreted literally by some, including Edgar Cayce. While never exactly condemned by the Christian Church, belief in reincarnation has always been highly discouraged. (Technically speaking, the condemnation of Origenism at the "Ecumenical" Council of Constantinople in 553 is of doubtful authority, since the Pope and the papal party refused to attend, and the majority of bishops present were Monophysites.)

In its simplest outline, reincarnation, first of all, presupposes the pre-existence of souls, that is, that all created, finite spirits had their beginning at the same "time." These are "embodied" throughout history in successive incarnations, the object of which is the progressive purification of the soul. (One of the strongest motives for belief in this doctrine is the mystery of evil and suffering; reincarnationist "karma" maintains that people suffer to atone for sins committed in previous lives, or, more positively, as an elected manner of purifying themselves.) Eventually, all human souls will be reunited to God in the spiritual perfection which He willed from the beginning, unless they have constantly chosen to seek deeper into evil. Nevertheless, a logical consequence of reincarnationism is the denial of the eternity of hell, which indeed goes against the grain of many of Jesus' utterances on that subject as well as traditional Christian doctrine. Still, many professed Christians believe in reincarnation in a modified way. The doctrine of purgatory is itself a kind of reincarnationism, since it is basically a belief that the soul can still atone for sin (be purified) after death.

To be sure, reincarnation takes some of the sting out of life in a cruel society, especially one in which many members die of hunger and disease because of over-population, such as India. But it also deprives the person of the importance of the moment, relativizing history and totally subjectifying the urgency of the Good News. The question, of course, remains a hard one: is the present life, with its absurdities and tragedies—where infants die in the womb and millions of innocent people are callously slaughtered, where starvation and disease and illiteracy are the common lot of mankind—the only chance for salvation? Here we touch on the greatest mysteries of life and religion, the answers to which can only be known with certainty on "the other side."

In the meantime, as we work out our salvation with fear and trembling, scientists and spiritualists are awaiting—and even hurrying—the dawn of mind. From the alpha-wave generators of San Francisco to the alchemical dens of Paris, man the magician-sage-priest, the eternal seeker, is discovering still new and exciting frontiers within his own cranium. Perhaps he will discover that the voices that speak from the past, as the "reincarnated" undergo hypnosis, are merely submerged parts of the conscious personality manifesting themselves. Or, on the other hand, he may discover something altogether different.

10.

Behind the Occult Revolution: A Place Called Anomie

In the basement of the LaSalle Street YMCA in Minneapolis, there is a coffee house called "Anomie." Nearby is one of the largest occult bookstores and "colleges" in the nation, the Gnostica School. However coincidental their proximity, there is symbolic irony herein, for from a sociological viewpoint, the occult revolution is a product of a disintegration of cultural norms and values which sociologists since Durkheim have labelled *anomie*. More specifically, contemporary occultism is symptomatic of a profound and far-ranging transformation of the entire socio-cultural system of the West, which gives the movement its pronounced religious character. The increasing rate of technological change, rapid shifts of structure, doctrine, and liturgy in the churches, political upheaval, and even natural disasters have combined to create a state of mind in many people, especially the young, which is nothing short of eschatological. We seem to be on the brink of either total chaos or the inauguration of a whole new aeon, a leap into the future. Whatever the outcome, occultism represents one way of responding to the stresses of future shock.

This chapter will concentrate on the "meaning" aspect of the occult revolution in terms of change and response, building on the idea that the emergence of counter cultures represents a reaction to anomic conditions in society, and that the ultimate values involved in current social transformations make that emergence pre-eminently a religious phenomenon. In the next chapter, some theological appraisals of the occult revolution will be made, followed by a consideration of the alternative responses suggested by the occult revolution as ways into a livable future.

Anomie and the Sacred Canopy

Many observers of contemporary society, among them theologians as well as behavioral scientists and philosophers, have traced the erratic course that has brought the human enterprise out of the doldrums of superstition and ignorance into the maelstrom of today's civil and religious life. Robert K. Merton, Margaret Mead, C. P. Snow, Buckminster Fuller, Marshall McLuhan, Paul Goodman, David Riesman, Jacques Ellul, Jacques Barzun, Arthur Koestler, William C. Whyte, Lewis Mumford, and many other thoughtful scholars point to the inescapable fact that Western civilization is now caught in the turmoil of too rapid social change. The cultural systems of both East and West, as a matter of demonstrable fact, are being pulled apart by the future shock of being thrust into the twenty-first century while still unable to cope with the left-over difficulties of the nineteenth.

The impact of social tension is readily identifiable today in the spheres of politics, both abroad and at home, in scientific "progress," and in religious life.

There is a word for the condition of social disruption characteristic of our era. It was coined in the wake of the Protestant Reformation as Europe began pulling itself together: "anomie." The sociological theorist Robert K. Merton popularized the use of the term over two decades ago, but it very appropriately designates our contemporary cultural malaise. "Anomie," he wrote, "is conceived as a breakdown in the cultural structure, occurring particularly where there is an acute disjunction between the cultural norms and goals and the socially structured capacities of members of the group to act in accord with them." Earlier in the book he had described anomie more simply as "a climate of reciprocal distrust . . . in which common values have been submerged in the welter of private interests."[1] Anomie is a condition of social disorganization marked by relative norm-lessness; while not primarily a psychological category, it undoubtedly produces feelings which have been described as "anomic."

The word "anomie" is derived from the Greek word for "law" or "norm"—*nomos*—with the privative "*a*," "without." While "normlessness" is perhaps the closest English equivalent, "lawlessness" expresses something of the same tenor. Certainly, the recent outcry for increased "law and order" is an appeal from a perceived state of anomic disintegration.

In a healthy society—that is, a socio-cultural system in which goals and norms are well-integrated to greater or less degree—the appropriate response is conformity, which is to say that the socially oriented person accepts both the means and the ends of his society and acts in accord with them. In a malintegrated society, conformity becomes dysfunctional. A breakdown in the means-ends relationship necessitates adaptive behavior, and Merton classifies the possible alternatives as innovation, retreatism, ritualism, and rebellion.

Innovative behavior seeks to achieve the goals of the society by new or commonly unacceptable means. Retreatism is a passive abandonment of both the goals and the traditional means of attaining them; it is equivalent to apathy. Ritualism is opposed to innovation; it canonizes the means but tacitly abandons the former goals, actually converting means into ends, or discounting whether or not the means are able to achieve their ends. Rebellion, finally, involves overt rejection of both the means and the ends of society, substituting new goals and norms. It is thus opposed to retreatism.

In a stable society, these modes of behavior would be deviant. However, when strains, tensions, and conflicts within society

[1] *Social Theory and Social Structure,* New York, 1968, pages 216, 163.

exert pressure for change, these forms of response enable individuals to tolerate the shifting of goals and institutionalized means. Obviously, from this perspective, innovation is the safest adaptive response, but innovators must face the entrenched opposition of the ritualist, the classical arch-conservative, and, as well, the numbed apathy of the retreatist. Further, he may encounter the impatient demands of the rebel, who, if he attempts to reestablish the whole order of society, may accurately be called a revolutionary. But when a society finds itself on the verge of total disintegration, rebellion is the only sane path to follow, and the innovator will be derided as a "weak sister" or a "liberal," standing in the path of the new order.

In view of the occult revolution, we are not dealing with rebellion as such, but more than likely with a hybrid form of ritualistic and innovative behavior. (This means, logically, that the phenomenon is not a revolution at all, but a conservative reaction, a view which I would in no way dispute.) The relationship of magic, religion, and "science" typical of those involved with occultism implies that in the face of the organized churches' inability to cope with the data and results of scientific "progress" and especially of technological overdevelopment, the hunger for transcendence has led many *back* to forms of "folk religion." Sociologists and historians of religion have amply demonstrated that the traditional function of religion is to shore up belief in the meaningfulness of the cosmos. In times of great social stress, such as that produced by different rates of change in various sectors of a social or cultural system, religion's conservative power is very appealing, and historically there is a "return to faith." This is especially so in times of war. The rise of pentecostalism in the past decade is a case in point, and occultism is another.

Occultism is indeed a form of religion, a folk-religion, especially so witchcraft and satanism and, for many, astrology (which is generally more of a folk-psychology). Modern witches take pains to establish links—no matter how tenuous—with paleolithic religions. Whereas their history and anthropology are wanting, their feelings are in tune with the times. Similarly, Anton LaVey and the young cultists of the Process Church leave no doubt that what they are about is the establishment of religion. Both witches and satanists concur with regard to another point; their religions fill a void created by the default of Christianity.

To equate modern occultism solely with an attempt to establish a new religion would be wide of the mark, although that is certainly a feature of the occult movement. Today occultism is a subcultural motif which incorporates both religious and secular elements—it is a protest against both Church and State, testifying to the disillusionment of a sizable number of the young with political programs of whatever stripe. It is a reaction against the pretensions of science. And it is a desperate bid, perhaps a last effort, to achieve the religious experience of union with the "divine" and a meaning-giving encounter with the forces at work in history, society, and nature. Occultism is a counter culture.

Counter Occulture

Since the publication of Theodore Roszak's *The Making of a Counter Culture* it has become customary to classify everything from rock festivals to bearded ideologues and bombings as "counter-cultural." With regard to occult cults, labelling the whole business is not to have dealt with it, for like similar social phenomena, occultism is also *more* than a counter culture. This is certainly true of the "Jesus freaks," pentecostal people, and bhakti yogis and other conglomerations of disaffiliated and sometimes hostile subcultural groups in the population.

The term "counter culture" apparently made its debut in Talcott Parsons' classic text *The Social System,* first published in 1951, Oberlin sociologist J. Milton Yinger precised the concept in his 1961 article "Contraculture and Subculture" in the *American Sociological Review,* and later it appeared again in Roszak's book.

Yinger suggested that the term is applicable "whenever the normative system of a group contains, as a primary element, a theme of conflict with the values of the total society, where personality variables are directly involved in the development and maintenance of the group's values, and wherever its norms can be understood only by reference to the relationships of the group to a surrounding dominant culture." Roszak more heatedly describes the counter culture in negative terms: "a culture so radically disaffiliated from the mainstream assumptions of our society that it scarcely looks to many as a culture at all, but takes on the alarming appearance of a barbaric intrusion." Both Yinger and Roszak regard the central genetic factor in the emergence of such a subcultural group to be a malintegrated cultural system, which produces more or less radical disaffiliation and various degrees of dissent on the part of the members of the group. Dominant personal leadership is characteristic of a counter-cultural group, which comes most truly into its own when it sees its task as a dramatic protest against the prevailing norms of the larger culture.

Today's flourishing occult groups admirably fulfill both Yinger's and Roszak's qualifications for admission to the rank of a counter culture.

First of all, it is highly significant that as church attendance in the major denominations consistently has dropped, both occult groups and splinter sects, representing the unorthodox and orthodox poles of disaffiliation, have grown enormously. Most occultists make no pretense that their adherence to whatever form of devotion or practice which they adopt is anything other than religious. Witchcraft, as we have seen repeatedly, is commonly regarded as "the old religion" by its practitioners. Members of the orthodox counterpart to occult cults, for instance pentecostal sects within the major denominations, are similarly striving to be more religious than the average parishioner. It is also important to note that many epiphenomena associated with pentecostalism, such as glossolalia, healing, and other "miracles," are also prominent in occult groups, indicating that these subcultures have more in common than their rejection of the larger groups' norms. They are opposite sides of the same coin.

Secondly, in addition to an active rejection of prevalent norms, occult subcultural groups rely greatly on charismatic leadership for organization and inspiration. Again, the same can be said for the pentecostal movement and sects such as the Children of God and the Holy Order of Mans, Shiloh, and the Hare Krishna "Back to Godhead" movement, most of which also share a pronounced eschatological spirit.

Finally, as has already been implied, occult counter cultural cults ("occultures") can and must be defined only in terms of the dominant culture. An essential requirement for any kind of revolution is an organized opposition. Thus LaVey's Church of Satan, no less than the Children of God, define themselves as opponents of the organized churches and the hypocritical norms of believers-at-large, the "gray people." But neither group would exist if it were not for the prior existence of their antagonists. Pentecostal groups, especially those within the Catholic communion, are not openly defiant of the Church, but it is nevertheless true that they have their own group identity, services, and so on. Within Merton's typology, we might characterize them as innovators whose new means are really old means—antedating everything but the event of Pentecost and the gifts of the Spirit.

It cannot be said that every occult group is counter cultural, especially those which history grants the protection of venerability, examples being the Rosicrucians, the Masons, the Order of the Golden Dawn, the Enthusiasts, and the Illuminati. Today, however, there is sufficient evidence to conclude that as a recent phenomenon, youth cults of unorthodox occult mein are in large measure elements of the counter culture.

Occultism is not simply a question of fashion, to anticipate another objection. Despite the inevitable outpourings of cosmetics, cheap jewelry, and games with occult-sounding names, a process which Roszak calls "commercial verminization," occultism functions primarily for its committed adherents as a religion, philosophy, ethics, and psychology—all on a "folk" level, that is, highly competent, skilled, but non-professional. This is partially explainable in terms of the economic level from which most converts to occultism are drawn (or, more accurately, drop out of)—for almost without exception, the occultures represent a middle or upper-middle-class membership. Many of these young cultists, as is again the case with the Children of God and some bhakti yogis, are former drug-users ("acid-heads"), disenchanted hippies and yippies, and runaways. Many older "flower children" are now members of witches' covens, which helps explain their characteristically non-aggressive attitude (granting the occasional "black" witch).

Projecting a possible outcome of the occulture's impact with organized religion and society in general is a grave temptation, assuming that contemporary society is all that predictable. Given the vacuum in religious commitment today, it is unlikely in the extreme that witch hunts and pogroms will be brought to bear against occult sectarians despite their opposition to the larger culture. Modern technocratic society has learned how to deal with counter-cultural opposition in far more effective ways than by creating martyrs. Roszak describes in detail how, by means of the media, fashion, and patronization, the technology simply absorbs the off-beat. Long hair and beads became the rage among the jet-set as the Days of Rage were landing the SDS rebels in Chicago jails. "Radical chic" was likewise a highly effective counter-revolutionary offensive. Similarly, zodiac charm bracelets and computerized horoscopes, witchcraft records, and situation comedies on television are efficient instruments of social exorcism.

Modern occultism may do some damage, psychologically and even physically, to those who adopt it as a way of life. On the other hand, witches discourage taking drugs, and satanists do not manufacture napalm or SSTs. If the occult movement is not co-opted by big business, it may survive long enough to function as a constructive critique of contemporary religion, science, and politics. Perhaps in fact, the social contribution of all counter cultures is to make the dominant culture self-conscious enough to address itself to its deficiencies. More positively, there is a promise of hope in occulture that lies not so much in its radical rejection of the norms and goals of society, valid though this may be, but more in the attempt and possibly the achievement of creating alternative, more consistently humane goals, and experimenting with new means to those ends. We may be on the verge of a breakthrough in an understanding of man's mind, about which we know so relatively little, and the occult revolution also seems to portend a spiritual awakening in society as a whole, which may result in a new alliance among three old foes.

Magic, Science, and Religion

Since the dawn of human civilization, religion, science, and magic have been associated in the often tensely charged field of man's understanding and aspirations. Their interfaces, although not a sufficient framework for humanity's progress, have been of paramount importance in the shaping of social and intellectual patterns of all cultures. In the interstices between the great achievements and the debasement of science and religion, the creative energies of mankind's mind and will seem to become manifest in mathematics, art, and literature. When in turn their force is at last spent, then come reformation and revolution—discoveries and inventions which inaugurate a new cycle. Magic seems to appear in the lull between the end of one cycle and the beginning of another, when the old is no longer good enough and the new is not yet.

From an "evolutionary" viewpoint, aided by the research of Professors Thorndike, Malinowski, Frazer, and Eliade, we may say with some assurance that magic and religion seem to have developed side by side, distinguished by their respective attitudes of either submission to or adoration of the mysterious powers of the universe or, conversely, a conscious will to subdue and direct the cosmic forces. A later development, science—like religion—manifests more of a reverential, contemplative attitude towards nature, while its utilitarian step-child, technology, applies scientific discoveries to the phenomenal world and thus resembles magic in its attempt to direct and manipulate the environment. Today's technician is kin to the sorcerer's apprentice, who disastrously applied forces beyond his understanding to reshape the world for his own convenience and pleasure.

In an era of superstition and magic, real science and true religion flourish only in protected enclaves—monasteries and secret laboratories. Such is the popular and not wholly inaccurate conception of Europe during the Dark Ages, and until recent times was the case in many regions of the earth. Contrariwise, when scientific progress and developed religious life prevail, magic as well as sheer technology loses its hold on men's minds, and the black arts continue in secret, as did alchemy for centuries. (Pauwels and Bergier in their work *The Morning of the Magicians* maintain that alchemists are still hunting for the philosophers' stone and the elixir of life.) Fortunately, this curious dialectic, which is traced with regard to astrology by Louis MacNeice in his excellent history of that subject, has preserved the valuable findings of the ancients until today, especially in the areas of pharmacy, physics, and chemistry.

Of course, it cannot be maintained that religion and science always prosper and decline simultaneously, much less magic and technology. Nevertheless, their progress seems closely interrelated.

It was not, for example, until the decline of the Middle Ages, which had witnessed the grandeur of high Christendom as well as the beginnings of a restored scientific mentality with the introduction of the Arabian commentaries on Aristotle by the scholastics, that magic, witchcraft, and superstition, abetted by the scourges of warfare and plague, arose once more to dominate even the burgeoning metropolises of northern Europe. Witchcraft, as we discovered, dates only from the fourteenth century.

The Renaissance, for all its splendor, was not really a period of great scientific or spiritual development, but rather one of technological hauteur and religious pretentiousness. Only with the Protestant Reformation and the Copernican revolution did religion and science revive. It was then that magic and blind credulity—including, in the opinion of the new thinkers, among them Erasmus, many of the extreme devotional practices of Roman Catholicism as well as its adherence to the Ptolemaic cosmos—became a target of extermination.

Restored by scientists of the caliber of Newton and Galileo, the New Thought overcame mere technology, which had amounted to little more than endless variations on medieval science. An age of invention and discovery was inaugurated. After the interminable wars of religion, pietism and the Tridentine reforms replaced the politically oriented and corrupt opulence of late medieval and Renaissance Catholicism (and also introduced new measures to eliminate witchcraft in Europe and America).

With the Enlightenment, new scientific achievements were replaced by philosophical permutations, which paved the way for the degrading technology of the Industrial Revolution. Religion again became the enemy of reason, and more than a century would elapse before the work of Darwin and Faraday, Newman and Schleiermacher (who were born within the space of thirty years of each other), would spark a new, faster cycle of the process.

Today, it is no great revelation to say that technology has again surpassed scientific research or that the pressures of the changing world have increased. But it is also true that we are living in an era when the rate of change has accelerated beyond a durable pace. As Alvin Toffler has pointed out, we have seen within the last decade at most a doubling back of the process of social change upon itself, a sort of McLuhan reversal. As time has been ever further compressed, we have begun to witness a sort of "recapitulation" of Western history in the space of a few years. Witches are deliberately reviving paleolithic rites, while communards attempt to establish neolithic villages in New Mexico; Edwardian styles and micro-skirts and, now, hot-pants, are almost equally fashionable; nostalgia is a party game while we worry about the year 2000. The world, so radically compressed, sometimes seems to be about to shatter, and that is the feeling of anomie, of future shock. And since mankind has traditionally fallen back on a magical view of the world when religion, political life, and science have been unable to secure the frame of the cosmos, it is not surprising that the occult has made its appearance at this time, precisely as a counter-cultural phenomenon.

As every counter culture depends on the larger group for the financial resources and material goods by which it lives, as well as a moral and political target against whose values, beliefs, and conduct alternative styles of life can be developed, such groups cannot be considered inimical to the best interests of society when it is in the tumult of major transformation. Rather counter cultures are an asset, an advance-guard seeking out new avenues of development and new goals for society. For such evolutionary exploring to succeed, it is perhaps necessary for society to provide opposition, for without some mutual polarity, truly alternative structures and modes of behavior would not develop, but merely blossom for a time as the conceits of fashion. Conversely, the possibility of total repression is more dangerous for the whole society than is mere patronization, for by suffocating the social systems of the future in their infancy, the society itself would be destroyed. Counter cultures must be enabled to succeed or fail on their own—which means without subsidization or persecution (there will be opposition enough without that)—for therein lies the very hope for tomorrow's world.

11.

Christ and the Powers

WHEN the son of the late Episcopal Bishop James Pike took his life in February of 1966, there began a series of incidents that not only profoundly reoriented the controversial cleric's own life, but also thrust into the public eye the religious dimension of the occult revolution. Contact with the dead has had many names—necromancy, spiritualism, spiritism, and so on—and although regarded as a particularly baneful form of un-Christian practice, it has recently received new attention by theologians and scientists. (A comprehensive bibliography of writings in this area can be found in an appendix to Bishop Pike's *The Other Side.*) It has also become a matter of concern to young occultists, whose seances have produced some uncommon experiences.

As Bishop Pike learned after he had "contacted" his son through the aid of several mediums—or, rather, after his son had contacted him in that manner—many Christians interpret quite literally the Bible's injunction against necromancy as a prohibition forbidding seances and any other attempts to "reach" the departed directly: "Do not have recourse to the spirits of the dead or to magicians; they will defile you" (Lev. 19, 31); "If a man has recourse to the spirits of the dead or to magicians, to prostitute himself by following after them, I shall set my face against that man and outlaw him from his people" (Lev. 20, 6); and "Any man or woman who is a necromancer must be put to death by stoning; their blood shall be on their own heads" (Lev. 20, 27). Letters reviling him for exposing himself to the power of Satan were directed to Pike by well-meaning people, and after his untimely death in the desert near Bethlehem, only three years later, there were many who saw in the affair the punishing hand of God.

Most objections to spiritualist seances come from Christians who have no doubts that the souls of the dead are either in heaven or hell. Their opposition is not aimed against belief in the survival of the soul beyond death (something Bishop Pike was skeptical about even after his son's death), but against the attempt to communicate with them, which is seen as a diabolical trap.

Here the paradox of the Church's attitude towards occultism becomes manifest: while professing belief in the communion of saints, and while affirming the real existence of disembodied spirits, traditional Christianity refuses to accept the possibility of a non-sinful approach to the souls of the dead other than prayers offered on their behalf and to them. And even though the Church has at times acknowledged that the dead (such as saints) have appeared to men, the dread of seances and condemnation of conjurations has gone on unabated.

As we noted earlier, the official representatives of organized religion never took kindly to the attempts of their rivals—magicians, seers, and their company—to duplicate feats which they themselves performed or at least believed in. Understandably so, for magic and occult practices have always been—and been recognized as—counter-religious behavior. Occasionally, such conduct actually became anti-religious, especially as venal purveyors of magical arts sold their services to ambitious monarchs and pontiffs. The crime of simony, now defined as traffic in sacred offices, originated with Simon Magus, a Samaritan magician who wanted to buy the power of conferring the Holy Spirit and performing miracles (Acts 8, 9–24). It did not take too many centuries of wealth and power for the successors of Peter, as well as emperors and kings, not only to sell positions of authority but to hire magicians and astrologers. Some popes were magicians themselves. Aside from the corruption of Church dignitaries, there was also a traditional fear among pastors and spiritual theologians that feats of power such as miracles could be achieved by demonic influence and they remained wary of anything extraordinary. So thoroughly was the mass of the faithful convinced of the reality of miracles (as well as of demons and the whole magical panoply), that reports of phenomena surpassing the "natural" were officially discounted in canonization processes unless they could withstand a rigorous investigation by a trained clerical lawyer appropriately titled "the devil's advocate." This, however, was a later development and largely the result of popular credulity.

Today, as the occult arts and sciences bloom again in what appears to be the decaying remains of Western civilization, and seances compete with protest demonstrations and football games for the allegiance of the young, it seems at least "relevant" to explore some of the theological aspects from an historical as well as contemporary perspective. Most of our theological evaluations of occult phenomena are derived from medieval and Renaissance interpretations in any case.

The Biblical View

In the Old Testament, the case against magicians, conjurers, astrologers, necromancers, seers, and the rest of that coterie seems completely damning. This much should be evident from the references scattered throughout the various chapters on witchcraft, magic, and satanism in particular. The Book of Leviticus is most explicit in the official denunciation of occultism, but throughout the historical books, particularly Samuel and Kings, and in the prophetic writings, especially Isaiah and Ezekiel, there are scathing satires on diviners and astrologers. Despite the injunctions and prohibitions, magic did not die out among the Chosen

People, but figured even in the development of Christian doctrine. (To be sure, while *"magos"* was the technical Greek word for magician, the most frequently used term, and always pejorative, was *"pharmakeus,"* from which we derive our word "pharmacist.") But needless to say, the apostles' attitude was no less severe towards sorcery than was that of the prophets of old.

We have already sampled the wrathful denunciations of Christian theologians of the patristic period—Origen, Augustine, Jerome, John Chrysostom—and found the early medieval missionaries such as Boniface and the Fathers of Auxerre stringent in their measures against witchcraft and sorcery. By the high Middle Ages, a theological synthesis was developed, most notably by St. Thomas Aquinas (1224–1274), which became the official attitude of the Church—both Catholic and (implicitly) Protestant.

The Thomistic Opinion

Thomas assumed a fairly unbending stance with regard to all forms of magic, especially divination, basing his arguments on Holy Writ and St. Augustine's *De Doctrina Christiana*. For both theologians, the attempt to divine the future by necromancy, augury, sortilege, astrology, or palmistry was superstitious and gravely sinful, for such practices attributed to natural agencies what was not within their sphere of causality and, more importantly, they represented an explicit or implied compact with demons, who could thus wreak their malice on humankind. In surprisingly strong terms, Aquinas thus answers a hypothetical objection: 'No temporal utility can compare with the harm to spiritual health that results from inquiry into the occult by the invocation of demons." He later describes the progressive enslavement to demonic power of the magician: "The operation of the demon inserts itself into those divinations which proceed from false and vain opinion so that men's minds can become entangled in vanity and falsehood." Calling on Augustine,

Aquinas writes further: "A good Christian should beware of 'mathematicians' [astrologers] and of all impious diviners, particularly of those who tell the truth, lest his soul, deceived by consort with demons become ensnared into their company."[1]

Thus, for Western Christianity, the book was shut on the subject for seven hundred years, although necromancy and all the varieties of magic and divination continued more or less unabated, surviving even the fiery persecutions of the seventeenth century.

An Alternative View

In the Renaissance, the witchcraft trials, extensive legislation and inflammatory sermons, tracts and debates among experts amply testify to the continuing belief in and disfavor of the power of demons who lure men into damnation through magic and witchcraft. To be sure, there were clergymen who delved into the magical arts even then, but the official position was never in doubt. Not until the nineteenth century did the ban begin to weaken (except within the Swedenborgian movement which began a century before). In England especially, clergymen began paying greater heed to psychic research—in France, Mesmer and Charcot had begun the long trek that would lead to the discovery of hypnotism as well as psychotherapy. Noted scientists and public figures such as Sir Arthur Conan Doyle, William James, and Henri Bergson became involved in psychic research as the century waned; Doyle in particular was a firm believer in spiritualism. In America, after the famous case of the Fox sisters of Hydesville, N.Y., there was also a veritable psychic revolution.

Throughout the northern hemisphere, scientists and philosophers were beginning to wonder if all the supernatural furor of the past thousand years was in fact based on natural, human powers, and even if contact with the departed was a possibility.

[1] See *Summa Theologiae* II–II, qq. 92–95; also *Comment. in Gen.* II, 17.

However, the rise and vindication of psychiatric psychology and behavioralism soon eclipsed interest in psychic phenomena for their own sake and as avenues into the secret parts of the mind, for the Freudians had discovered the unconscious, which could be relied on to explain almost everything. Even Carl Jung, who of all the new psychologists was most open to a critical evaluation of the occult, found in it primarily a support for his theories of the collective unconscious and the archetypes.

In 1937, however, the Church of England approved a report which dealt with spiritualistic matters. It had been submitted at the request of the Archbishops of Canterbury and York, although they perhaps had no intention of making the findings known to the public. Nevertheless, in 1946, the report was "leaked," and many Anglican clergymen were soon openly claiming mediumistic abilities. On the Catholic side, Father Herbert Thurston, a Jesuit of the Bollandist school, was meanwhile studying poltergeist phenomena and cases of demonic seizure from a keenly analytic point of view. His *Ghosts and Poltergeists* remains a classic work on this subject.

Possibly the most comprehensive accounts of recent theological interest in the area of spiritualism and psychic phenomena are in Bishop Pike's *The Other Side* and *If This Be Heresy*. He very carefully distinguishes between the desire to "use" the dead for knowledge of the future and the desire to communicate with them across the unknown barrier between life and afterlife. He makes his own attitude as a theologian quite clear: "It would seem that many of those who for years have been mouthing the words 'I believe in . . . the Communion of Saints . . . the Resurrection of the Body; and the Life everlasting' and have been purporting to accept scriptural passages about these themes, including the communication of Jesus with his disciples, either do not really believe them or have never thought about their meaning at all. If the Church is to continue to make such affirmations, one would hope that more enlightened Church members will begin to take into account the rapid accumulation of scientific data which are supportive of them. If not, the Church may find itself in a very awkward position of being less believing with regard to some of its basic doctrinal tenets than secularists who have objectively examined factual evidence pointing to their truth."[2]

Today, as accounts of miracles, demonic possession, and other "supernatural" events are less and less well-received by Scripture scholars and theologians, the likelihood of "natural" explanations for the phenomena themselves is becoming stronger. ESP and mental powers such as psychokinesis and telepathy are no longer regarded by scientists as so much gobbledegook from the ages of superstition and religious frenzy. At the same time, and more to the point in the present context, supernaturalism itself is making something of a "comeback" in recent religious thought, as for instance in sociologist Peter Berger's *A Rumor of Angels*. As we have likewise already seen, the pentecostal movement, faith-healing, glossolalia, and xenoglossy are as much a part of parish life in the United States and Latin America as Holy Name societies and sodalities were a few years ago. (The identical phenomena appear in occult sects, as well, a fact which has yet to create any real friction between the "Jesus freaks" and "devil worshippers," perhaps because they are as yet unaware of the irony of it all.) From a pastoral viewpoint, a reassessment of supernaturalism is a theological imperative, especially if John Henry Newman's *consensus fidelium* argument is to have further meaning to the post-Vatican II world.

Perhaps the most impressive of recent developments in the contrapuntal progress of popular religion—if not the most profound—is the emergence in the midst of the counter culture of groups of young people derisively called "Jesus freaks." Their appearance was conceivably inevitable, but it was no less surpris-

[2] *The Other Side,* Garden City, 1968, pages 291–292.

198

ing when placards at demonstrations were discovered reading "Jesus Loves *You!*" or to be confronted (as I was) in midtown Chicago by twoscore and ten Children of God robed in sackcloth and wearing ashes in their hair, silently marching back from a pray-in during the Days of Rage.

The Jesus People

When Billy Graham's Crusade appeared in Chicago recently, the thousands of middle-class, white, suburban citizens who attended found themselves greeted outside of McCormick Place not by war protestors (nor even by emissaries from the Church of Satan), but by placard-carrying "Jesus freaks" hawking their underground newspaper. Within the last two years, the Jesus movement has become a powerful cadre in the counter culture, from the militant protests of the Children of God to the spiritually frenetic Jesus-rock festivals which are now rivalling the secular concerts. Rice and Webber's *Jesus Christ Superstar* has become a best-selling album, and several companies are touring with multi-media and live concert versions of the rock opera. (The Kansas City production, imperiled by a last-minute copyright suit, received national attention in May 1971, gaining even the cover story of *Life* magazine in the following week.) When the record set was first released in England, it quickly achieved international stardom among the young, its nearest rival being (significantly) *Black Sabbath,* a rock celebration of sorcery and witchcraft. Such irony is not accidental—the Jesus phenomenon, like the emergence of pentecostalism on college campuses and in suburban parishes, is as much a part of the eschatological occult revolution as is the revival of magical cults, less an index to a spiritual awakening than a sign that the young are truly aware that something has gone wrong with the world.

It is tempting to suggest that popular religious enthusiasm, especially when blessed by the entrepreneurs of the entertainment world, represents a form of future shock-therapy. As Cecil B. De Mille and his imitators perceived, catering to the religious impulses of mass audiences without requiring anything so radical as conversion or repentance is highly lucrative, particularly if the producer can squeeze in several sex scenes and a lot of gore. Both pandering and exploitation in the religious zone of human feelings remind us, nevertheless, that the religious impulse is both highly sensitive and pervasive, rooted, as Jung maintained, in the depths of the psyche. When Buick ads offer "something to believe in," something precious in the human spirit is being affirmed, no matter how basely. So also with Jesus-rock. The testimony is valid, regardless of the producers' motives.

Cynicism comes too easy in the modern world, however, and it is possible to explore this outpouring of cultural religious lyricism without assuming bad faith on anyone's part. It goes back, no doubt, to Gospel jazz, the "soul" music of Ethel Waters and Mahalia Jackson, which, in turn, was the expression of the searing trials of faith in the black community of the South. Such Gospel music appeared in the glorious sound of the Edwin Hawkins' Singers "Oh Happy Day," and hovers in the background of Simon and Garfunkel's "The Boxer" and especially throughout the album *Bookends*. The Rotary Connection's style of acid-rock owes much to Gospel music, and it has influenced Judy Collins, whose recording of "Amazing Grace" became a quick success, having made its contemporary reappearance in the film *Alice's Restaurant*. Even Oral Roberts and Billy Graham have benefitted from folk hymns, and Tennessee Ernie Ford ranks near them in the evangelistic drive of his songs.

Eastern influences added to the identification of rock and religion; the Beatles certainly popularized Oriental mysticism in lyrics even before their rupture, and George Harrison's "My Sweet Lord" made the connection with Jesus explicit. Ravi Shankar and the Maharishi Yogi were evident enough to provide a tacit confirmation of the new syncretism.

The leap from Norman Greenbaum's "Spirit in the Sky" to *Jesus Christ Superstar* is not a great one; what made the transition from allusion to affirmation (although the opera is thoroughly anti-supernatural) was the eruption onto the scene of the Jesus freaks themselves. Like many witches and satanists, they were in many cases drop-outs, acid-droppers, disfranchised militants, and runaways who found in Jesus, rather than in their Buick dealer, "someone to believe in" and turn on to. And they did.

Not all of the new Jesus-movement sects would countenance the demythologized Christ of the rock opera; many are stridently anti-cultural—one is reminded of the bands of desert monks who occasionally rampaged through Alexandria in the early days of Christianity. And perhaps not unduly, for these sects represent a flight into the desert to await the End as much as did the monastics of Egypt. Apocalyptic eschatology is ready to their speech and permeates their music and writing. And no man-geared calamity will do for them; the Children of God, for example, are prepared for the coming of Jesus Christ on clouds of glory to judge the living and dead. We are living, they say, in the final age, for the devil is manifestly triumphant in the world. And thus we return to one of the major themes of the occult revolution, the millennial reappearance of the belief that the Last Day is at hand, that the world is coming to an end, or as Mama Cass sings, that "There's a New World Comin'."

On Eschatology

Georges Cuvier, the father of vertebrate paleontology, was startled to learn in the declining years of the eighteenth century that his native France had been alternately inundated and elevated in three successive periods of geological transformation, separated by thousands of years. Glacial ages have, in addition, repeatedly entombed the northern hemisphere under miles of ice, gouging canyons, valleys, and basins where rivers and lakes would one day be the left-overs of mighty glaciers. Continents have been raised and have sunk beneath the oceans, split apart and drifted away from the central land mass. Enormous meteors have collided with the earth, and if the theories of Immanuel Velikovsky are correct, even planets have narrowly missed destroying the world.

Mankind's memory is comparatively short. There is evidence that our ancestors walked the land more than two million years ago, and yet written records date back hardly farther than five thousand years. There are no accounts of the ice ages or of other disasters—unless, of course, the stories of the Deluge and similar catastrophes that figure in the folklore of almost every people are taken to be indicative of some proto-historical fact. Such cataclysms, according to myths and legends, nearly destroyed life on earth; had it not been for God's intervention, everything would have perished.

We believe today that the earth is quiet, that volcanoes are unpleasant anachronisms, and that earthquakes are unfortunate disasters. We are quite sure that the upheavals that created the mountains are over, and that the huge earth will continue to absorb our insignificant waste forever if need be. How often do we think that we could be living in the interstices between glacial periods or that a totally devastating geological "accident" such as the reversal of the poles (which happened some millions of years ago) might reoccur? If we do have such paranoid thoughts, we see a psychiatrist or at least hope that God will intervene and save us.

It seems likely that the religious experience of salvation from greater or lesser global catastrophes (what could be more ultimate?) formed the eschatological element of the world's great faiths. In the Judaeo-Christian tradition, such a view of history-- God's miraculous interventions and his ultimate eschatological triumph—is central to the proclamation of the Gospel. The immediacy of Christ's return became an article of faith for the early Christians, and even after a thousand years the belief had not died out completely. We still proclaim in our creeds that Jesus "will come again in glory to judge the living and the dead," and from the proclamations of the counter-cultural evangelists today it seems clear that another thousand years has not eroded completely the vision of the Last Judgment and the end of time.

Such a view of things is difficult to reconcile with a workaday attitude towards life, much less a "scientific" view of the world such as Bultmann cherishes. It is consequently not surprising that the rebellious and innovative Jesus freaks and Process People have eschewed both to a great extent—becoming "religious" in the old sense of the word (as in "religious order") and literal in their interpretation of Scripture. To be sure, their Sunday school and catechism classes admirably prepared them for that, but it took a major breakdown in the cultural system to bring it forth.

What that breakdown was has been explored in the chapter on anomie; how it was experienced can be best illustrated by returning to *Hair*. With the "Flesh Failures," *Hair*'s exuberance, which has slowly been turning into a kind of unsettling fury, changes into a scream of pessimistic cynicism, as the once hope-filled flower children approach the dusk of Pisces,

> *facing a dying nation*
> *of moving paper fantasies,*
> *listening for the new-told lies*
> *with supreme visions of lonely tunes . . .*

Hair lets us know what is destroying the fabric of hope that should be the guideline of youth—the war, the rape of the environment, the rending asunder of the generations and the family, government lies, distrust of adults, the very rootlessness of youth. Even the Church is mocked, in a curiously ambivalent way, and most particularly by Woof, who is a pathetically moving portrayal of the Christian-trained homosexual ("Sodomy"). The

Church, too, has failed us; if indeed God is dead, it is because He surrendered himself to human frailty ("Manchester, England"). Science is a willing slave to the military ("Three-five-zero-zero") and a threat to human indecency (a cherished value among the Tribe: "The Flesh Failures"). Thus there is nothing left to live for, except the Tribe itself, which Claude abandons when he chooses not to burn his draft card. He is inducted and then rejected by the Tribe, who leave his corpse on the wintry stage as they move off to nowhere ("Let the Sun Shine In").

Many of those to whom *Hair* was a living reality—the radically disaffiliated youngsters who had dropped out of society by the thousands to seek samadhi in "the Haight" or the communes of Taos—eventually adopted the magical attitude foreshadowed by the Tarot magician dominating center stage. For occultism is an escape from the crushing depersonalization of contemporary life; it reaffirms the worth of the individual, promising him knowledge kept secret for aeons and power over his destiny and the lives of others. Magic is, in the final analysis, an ideology, a whole way of life fraught with religious dynamism. Like religion itself, magic (as Malinowski insists) is "not merely a doctrine or a philosophy, not merely an intellectual body of opinion, but a special mode of behavior, a pragmatic attitude built up of reason, feeling and will alike."[3] Richard Cavendish finds in magic "a titanic attempt to exalt the stature of man, to put man in the place which religious thought reserves for God."[4]

Hence the terrible anger of the prophets against sorcery, which they—and the Judaeo-Christian tradition—identified with idolatry. For the magician to attempt to know the future or to dictate the course of events was to usurp the providence of God, to make himself into a god—that is, into an idol. Even the ancient prophets of Israel seem to have realized that sorcery was

[3] *Magic, Science and Religion*, pages 24–25.
[4] *The Black Arts*, New York, 1968, page 1.

baneful not merely because it poached on the preserves of a wrathfully jealous Lord, being a form of perverse worship, but because in that liturgical inversion the cultists themselves fell prey to the deadening power of the no-gods:

> *They have mouths but speak not;*
> *They have eyes but see not;*
> *They have ears but hear not,*
> *nor is there breath in their mouths.*
> *Their makers shall become like them,*
> *so shall everyone who trusts in them.*
> *(Psalm 135, 15–18)*

Demonic possession need not be dramatic and horrible to be real, and there is reason to be wary of the psychological influence which a reliance on occultism can exercise over the young in particular. The demonic, Rollo May writes, "is any natural function which has the power to take over the whole person."[5] Like Jung and the members of the Process Church, May finds that belief in demons outside the person are projections of our inner experience, which shuns direct responsibility for the anger, passion, and hatred that are a part of man's psychological endowment along with the powers of love, zeal, and creativity. When one element of the personality permanently dominates the whole, psychosis—demonic possession—results. The pressures of contemporary life impel many towards severe anxiety, and one way to escape is to allow the magical tendencies of the personality to take over, particularly because the demonic in man is "the enemy of technology."[6] Hence the radical opposition of contemporary occultism to the technocratic way of life; the drive of the human psyche to be in tune with the world of nature has been superseded by the claims of an automated, cybernetic, technological life dominated by the punch-clock. That is why

[5] *Love and Will,* New York, 1969, page 123.
[6] *Ibid.,* page 127

it should not have been surprising when some Canadian students destroyed a computer; violence is the demonic run amok.

If, then, occultism can be seen as a counter-cultural folk religion based on magic in conscious and unconscious reaction against the technocratic domination of the modern world and in the absence of religious support from the organized churches, there is some cause to be concerned about the welfare of the new occultists. For deprived of the balancing influences of authentic tradition and the conflicting political interests of various groups (pluralism, in other words), the new sectaries run a grave risk of being trapped in ideological postures of extreme reaction and ritualism. Values uncritically accepted as absolute easily harden into creeds, which combined with organizational structure and behavioral patterns create monolithic institutions. The acceptance of both the beliefs of the cults and the discipline imposed on prospective converts necessitates a certain conformity to expectations of what the ideal image of the members should be. And this type of image, institution, and ideology is the manifest presence of the demonic in society, whether cultural or counter-cultural.

The Principalities and Powers

Idolatry as well as sorcery led the Chosen People into slavery to demonic forces—demonic because they were possessive and destructive, and certainly forceful in the power by which the idols fascinated their adorers. The psychological dimension of this enslavement was not unnoticed by St. Paul, who throughout his ministry warned the infant Churches against the enticements and threats of the "principalities and powers" that were so inimical to Jesus and his Spirit. These forces were not merely the "demons" of popular imagination, but included everything hostile to Christ which could exercise control over the minds and hearts of men, depriving them of the true freedom possible only

206

through "the obedience of faith"—steadfast loyalty to the one God and Father of all.

Today the principalities and powers are still found wherever men are enslaved in mind or spirit by ideologies, institutions, or images of their own or others' making. Among modern theologians who have explored this Pauline theme with regard to contemporary society are William Stringfellow, a distinguished Episcopalian layman, and Heinrich Schlier, a German Catholic Scripture scholar.[7]

Images abound in the world of advertising, but they are far more pervasive than visual symbols. Primarily psychological entities, or "mental pictures," images may represent a person's own self-expectations as well as his expectations of others. The Freudian "ego ideal" is an image, and so are stereotypes, roles, categories, and "offices." Jung's archetypes are unconscious images shared by the race as a whole. Each image, from that of "the man in the gray-flannel suit" to the "radical," as well as ideals such as "the perfect housewife" or "the playmate of the month," are powerful inducements to conformity, and the power they exert is often tangible—in the choices we make at election time, in the products we buy, and in the frustration we feel when we realize that we are not "measuring up." They impel us to act in specific ways, from the cultivation of an artificial accent to the latest fashion in swimwear. No one is immune from the force of images.

Institutions are easily recognized for the power which they wield over men in today's world—whether the State, the university, the Boy Scouts, a political party, or even the Church itself. All institutions demand conformity to their standards—for instance, bureaucratic behavior in governmental agencies. It can be

[7] William Stringfellow, *Free in Obedience,* New York, 1964; Heinrich Schlier, *Principalities and Powers in the New Testament,* New York, 1961.

seen in the extensive supervision which modern corporations have over their employees' lives, especially executives, as William C. Whyte documented in *The Organization Man.* Stepping beyond the prescribed (but often tacit) limits imposed by institutions brings down on the head of the transgressor the full weight of social pressure which is most painfully felt in the affective zone ruled by the need for social approval. The greatest institutional system in the world is society itself, a haunting realization probed in the fiction of Kafka.

Ideologies also require conformity of belief and behavior. They are especially powerful in the creation and maintenance of value systems, whether political, religious, scientific, professional, or social. Here we find the -isms: capitalism, Marxism, Catholicism, Nazism, ritualism, patriotism, and so on. And it is here that we find the primary influence of occultism, which—as in the case of the others—when it begins to diminish a person's free self-disposition to life, controlling responses and filtering perceptions, becomes an instrumentality of the great principality (or *archon*) Death, whose power is the sway of sin.

Though such "principalities" are not personal, they are none-theless real, just as social relationships are real despite their im-materiality. Further, they are not "evil" in themselves (to a Christian, nothing is that), but their ability to restrict freedom and enforce conformity are hostile to the independence and creativity that man needs for truly communal brotherhood as well as personal liberty. Demonic images, institutions, and ideologies are often ranked against qualities at the heart of Christian life: love, service, openness to the future, forgiveness, and repentance.

Christ, in the thought of St. Paul, has by his passion and glorification subjected the principalities and their powers to himself, definitively breaking their hold on humankind by conquering the archon of death: "Then comes the End, when he delivers the kingdom to God the Father after destroying every prin-

208

cipality and every power and every force [domination]. For he must reign until he has put all his enemies under his feet. The last enemy to be destroyed is death" (1 Cor. 15, 24–26). In Ephesians 1, 20, Paul praises "the strength of his [God's] power at work in Christ, when he used it to raise him from the dead and to make him sit at his right hand, in heaven, far above every principality, power, virtue, or domination, or any other name that can be named, not only in this age, but also in the age to come." Again, "He has overridden the Law, and cancelled every record of the debt that we had to pay; he has done away with it by nailing it to a cross; and so he got rid of the principalities and powers, and paraded them in public, behind him in his triumphant procession" (Col. 2, 14–15).

Insofar as we are conformed to Christ rather than being ruled by the spirit of this world, we too are freed from the power of the principalities which, although defeated by Christ, still exercise control over the world by the consent of man. Thus Paul could write to the Colossians, "If you have really died to the principles [*stoicheion*] of this world, why do you still let rules dictate to you, as though you were still living in the world?" (Col. 2, 20). Paul characterizes the struggle to overcome sin in the life of the Christian as a cosmic conflict: "For I am sure that neither death, nor life, nor angels, nor principalities, nor things present, nor things to come, nor powers, nor height, nor depth, nor anything else in all creation, will be able to separate us from the love of God in Christ Jesus our Lord" (Rom. 8, 38–39). He "projects" the worldly principals into the total environment, but never indulges in crude anthropomorphism: "It is not against human enemies that we have to struggle, but against the principalities and powers who originate the darkness of this world, the spiritual army of evil in the heavens" (Eph. 6, 12).

Environmental forces, as Edward Hall and Marshall McLuhan tirelessly remind us, are nearly always "invisible," but they exercise a proportionately more pervasive power over us for all that. It is only when some shock disturbs our normal perceptions of the universe that the structures of our existence become manifest; for Paul, his encounter with Christ transformed his entire life. Often even psychics and mediums, as well as shamans and witch-doctors, discover their mysterious powers after an illness or injury or some psychological trauma. Life is never quite the same afterwards, but teaching others "to see" is a difficult and thankless task, as Plato indicated in the allegory of the cave. In the technological milieu in which we live and move and have our being, occultism itself can shock us out of our somnambulance as we once again come in contact with primitive magic and superstitions. But it is nevertheless true that occultism itself can have a hypnotic influence over its advocates, depriving them of the freedom that they had sought outside of the technocracy.

Perhaps the greatest danger in occultism is the sophistication with which technological man can approach it. Freed, he assumes, from the claims of superstition and supernaturalism, he is at first fascinated and then mystified by the answers of the ouija board or the Tarot deck. It all makes sense, somehow—astrology, crystal-gazing, palmistry . . . Is it only when we begin to encounter teenagers on the brink of hysteria because of an ouija board's prediction of immanent death or read of the ritual murders of Hollywood personalities or find the mutilated remains of sacrificial animals that we begin to explore our fears?

The literature of occultism grows daily, most of it merely sensational. But occasionally, we are struck by accounts of events that chill the blood—and this is the felt presence of the spirit of death.

The psychopathological transfer of occult eschatological fears to an innocent victim was emblematically recreated in the grotesque and tragic story of Bernadette Hasler, a seventeen-year-old Swiss girl tortured and beaten to death by a sect of religious fanatics in 1966. Bernadette had become the target for the maniacal persecutions of a defrocked German priest and his mistress, their febrile imaginations having been inflamed by the pseudo-mystical "revelations" of a Carmelite nun, Sister Stella, who was convinced that an apocalyptic disaster was about to befall the world. Bernadette, the daughter of a Swiss farmer on whose property the cult had established itself—a normal, cheerful girl—was singled out for punishment because of her imputed dealings with the devil. Systematically, the girl was abused and degraded physically and mentally until she half-believed and actually confessed to the fabrications. She was then beaten mercilessly, sometimes twice daily, until after months of such torture, and by then a pitiable lunatic, she died following an unusually severe thrashing at the hands of six of the "righteous" cultists. For their crime of inhuman cruelty, the main perpetrators of the cult were sentenced to ten years in prison, the lesser accomplices to four years or less.

Such incidents are not rare, despite the peculiar ugliness of the Hasler murder. The Tate-LaBianca killings at the hands of Charles Manson's "witches" revealed a similar pattern of eschatological fears, messianic delusions, sexual sadism, and cultic organization. In all, at least eleven persons died as a result of Manson's megalomaniacal pontifications, during the course of which he announced (and perhaps believed) that he was—simultaneously—Jesus Christ and Satan. Yet Manson was declared sane. Was he possessed? From a technical viewpoint, it is not likely; that he was in the power of a "demonic" force, completely under the sway of his own diseased self-image and the weird ideology that he espoused, cannot easily be discounted.

The Last Archon

We live in the realm of death. Despite the mounting birth rate in the world, we are mocked by the casualty lists from Asian conflicts and the Mideast. Earthquakes and storms bear off many thousands each year, while disease and hunger kill hundreds of thousands more. Accident and age kill; there are homicide and suicide. The "exploding population," the dearth of food and the means of its distribution portend famine for literally millions of people; the assault on the environment by unrestrained technological hubris also spawns death in the air we breathe and the water we drink. And, indeed, every man—every living thing— must in the proper time die his death. Man is, in his totality, his fallenness, as Heidegger says, a "being towards death." Death seems to be the ultimate reality of the universe.

Every religion and every philosophy of man is an attempt either to overcome death or to find meaning in it. Faith in the revelation of Jesus means that there is one and only life-assuring belief—"I have come that you might have life and have it more abundantly." For a Christian, all other claims and the works of man's hand and mind are only a mockery of the human longing for everlasting life. "He who strives to secure his life shall lose it." Therefore, every false allegiance and service is idolatrous, unwitting homage to the very power and sting of death.

In the thought of Paul, especially as interpreted by Schlier and Stringfellow, all the principalities and powers are acolytes of death; they promise but cannot achieve the gift of life. Our struggle against them must begin with ourselves. Self-love is the enemy of the self-less obedience of faith, which manifests itself primarily in loving service to our fellow men. But if we make our self-image the god of our idolatry through insecurity, self-seeking, ambition, jealousy, lust, envy—in short, as long as we direct our energies selfwards, we can never effectively break through the enslaving control of institutions and ideologies and least of all enable others to do so. We have already lost.

Insofar as astrology, palmistry, witchcraft, and other occultist beliefs answer a need for security and order amid a chaotic world, the freeing message of the Gospel will fall on deaf ears. We must learn that our only security comes from our loving trust in the Father, who alone can save. Every other form of security (or salvation, actually) is not only deceptive but idolatrous, for it attributes to creatures—no matter how powerful—what belongs to the Creator alone.

Real faith means not only enduring chaos, absurdity, and uncertainty in this world, ruled as it is by principalities and powers still warring against us, but doing so willingly, affirming our reliance on God alone, celebrating our debility and weakness as the opportunity for God to work through us and in us. We must affirm life as it is—an intense struggle of life against death, but we celebrate knowing that in Christ the definitive victory has been inaugurated and is now being carried to completion in his Holy Spirit.

The response of faith to the occult revolution is not some sort of counter-revolutionary strategem—witch hunts and persecutions, whether physical or psychological, have been revealed by history to be a heightening of the power of death in the world. Institutionalized religion easily becomes a principality when its own existence is threatened.

Rather, a vital Christian witness alone can counteract the power of death in the world. Mere presence is sufficient; the Church has as its principal task merely to be the Church. Thus we can avoid the tragic error of categorizing modern occultism as the work of Satan, for like all worldly phenomena it is a mixture of helpful and injurious elements. For many, occultism provides a refuge from the struggles within the Church itself, and it also serves to remind us of what the Church should be.

Christian Anarchy

Christians were early accused of the very sin that we so easily lay at the feet of modern magicians. Insofar as they refused to worship the State gods of the empire (having only One themselves), they were considered atheistic and idolatrous. Indeed, the Christian is an anarchist in that respect—he has only one archon, Jesus Christ; and only one God, the Father. He has been freed by Christ from the claims of all other archons and gods: "For although there may be so-called gods in heaven or on earth —as indeed there are many "gods" and many "lords"—yet for us there is one God, the Father, from whom are all things and for whom we exist, and one Lord, Jesus Christ, through whom are all things and through whom we exist" (1 Cor. 8, 5).

The implications of that belief are enormous; for the Christian, nothing may stand between him and the Father and Christ—no loyalty, no fear, no expectation, no promise or pledge. No nation or institution can demand such obedience, not even the Church. Thus the Christian has a vocation to be an anarchist, relativizing every image, institution, and ideology, every value and belief, every allegiance and desire with regard to the absolute love of God.

Sheer anarchism, to be sure, tends to become an ideological bias and nihilistic, not a genuine liberation from law but an escape from responsibility and freedom. As an ideology, it is a principality and leads to bondage. Christian anarchy is quite different; it is the prophetic drive to see everything in relation to the will of God. That in itself is a more difficult vocation than sheer anarchism, for the world does not like to occupy second place. But when the world threatens to come between the Christian and the love of God, there can be no other place for it. Otherwise the Christian anarchist, unlike his secular counterpart, is content to live at watchful peace with lawful authority and the manifold principalities.

Organized religion may well appear to the young as having failed to give meaning and fulfillment to life and therefore to be a principality of death. But to abandon organized churches to search for transcendence and an understanding of life's mysteries in the realm of the occult may involve an implicit surrender to powers beyond their comprehension and control, and which are no less inimical to freedom and joy. It is a frightening thing to attempt to choose between such alternatives.

James A. Pike was for many a living symbol of the contemporary Christian's pilgrimage towards an ever deeper understanding of the ultimate mystery of life. Yet he was able to remain faithful to his Church while wandering the labyrinth of occult theories, claims, and experiences. His example may prevent others from plunging over the edge of the unknown in their quest. Time will tell.

12.

Mystics and Mod Jesters

THE "old religion," as witches prefer to call their craft, is at-tractive to modern youth not because it is a new, liberal church, but simply because it is old and because it is highly religious. Young Catholics in particular seem to have found those qualities most appealing, as Hans Holzer relates, although he misses the whole point of the revival of witchcraft as a religious experience in his book *The Truth About Witchcraft*. The craft also pro-vides, it is true, a depth of sensual involvement and group solidarity that the organized churches have lost, and therein lies the clue to several pastoral alternatives for a more effective religious renewal, a sorely needed program in light of contem-porary social turbulence. For whether we relish the category or not, religion is the manifestation of a profoundly conservative impulse in man—the will to conserve his rootedness in nature and history and human fellowship. Such is also the burden—and glory—of mere Christianity insofar as it, too, is a religious move-ment in history. Yet Christianity is not a religion precisely, how-ever great its religious benefits are for Christians. It is more than a religion; as Teilhard de Chardin might have said, it is the core reality of mankind's thrust into the future, as much a liber-ating force as a conservative principle. Christianity is essentially and pre-eminently a revolution—a forward movement of a people in time achieved by a constant recapitulation of all that has been. We relive the past in the present as we create a future that is simultaneously novel and the product of the collective experience of mankind.

Membership in the Church—which is an organic reality—is and should be a religious experience, for it is a matter of ultimate concern for its members. Yet this cannot be allowed to change Christianity into a mere religion, an exclusively conservative system of dogmatic and cultic formulas and practices, dominated by rubricians and theological technicians. A corporate entity such as a church needs a government, it is true, and its central beliefs must be clear, its worship distinctive; the trial of the Church here is to prevent institutionalism and legalism from dominating its life, which can be achieved only by emphasizing service, communion, and the prophetic word. Thus, under the impetus of the guiding Spirit, whose task it is to reform the Church at all times, the growth of theocratic principality can be avoided.

The struggle for freedom against the principalities and powers of worldly power, prestige, wealth, and dominion creates a continual crisis in the lives of Christians. In the midst of the inner purification of the Church, however, deeply felt human needs may be overlooked, and consequently the fearful, the doubting, the self-righteous as well as the timid, may once again go "a-whoring" after the false gods of security, relevance, and orthodoxy, those contemporary flesh-pots and onions of captivity, the mud-plasters and band-aids on the sacred canopy.

It was not by accident that Esalen, T-groups, and "sensitivity training" appeared alongside of the flower children's crusade back to nature and the beginnings of the occult revolution. (The proper word for a medium in spiritualistic circles is, significantly, a "sensitive.") All followed hard upon the introduction of computertronics, cybernetics, automation, and microminiaturization into the mainstream of contemporary life. Even the recent ecological backlash is essentially a reaction against the untrammeled exploitation of the natural world—the devouring of resources, possibly uncontrollable automotive and industrial pollution of air and water, the mass slaughter of animal and plant species, the devastation of wilderness areas, and the flight from the cities. There is a growing awareness that by burying land equivalent to the state of Georgia under highways and parking lots and producing cars more than half as fast as we produce babies is altering the quality of life for the worse. The gauge of the defuturization of the American people is the hopelessness which they express when even attempting to cope with alternative courses of action. Technological mankind—not merely technicians (who seem to enjoy some kind of professional immunity), but the masses of citizens who are beneficiary to technical overdevelopment—is increasingly alien not only to personal encounter but to the whole of nature as well.

The impact of such a schizoid existence on the liturgical life of the Church has been profoundly negative. Already saddled with an ever-shifting pile of rubrical debris, the celebrating Church is also carrying on its back the bewildered mass of its Sunday visitors while being pulled by progressives and reactionaries in opposite directions. The ultimate straw hovering over its dromedarian back may be the realization that our jettisoned baggage—rituals, bells, incense and the like—have been reclaimed by the cultists of the occulture.

Not only are these new sects essentially intimate religious associations, they are highly sensitive to the fact that colors, fragrances, touch, the rhythms of dance, and the melodic paths of chant and hymnody constitute the material content of celebration. Such elements are selected not only because they evoke a mood of mystery and beauty, but because they are enjoyable in themselves and serve to identify the worshippers through sensual experience with the world beyond, the profane milieu as well as the "other" dimensions of reality. The powerful dual thrust of such times, instruments, places, and roles necessitates consecration: their being set aside for such exclusive liturgical employment.

In archaic and primitive religions, the articles and instruments of sacred service were always thus hallowed and restricted (or protected) from profane use. The month of February is named for the Roman *februa,* the sacred cleaning utensils of ritual purification used in homes and public buildings prior to the celebration of the new year. After their unique service, these brushes and pans were stored away in a suitably holy (that is, safe) place until the following spring.

The re-emergence in the counter-cultural churches of the consciousness of the sacred character of artifacts—which does not demand that they be expensive but simply reserved for exclusive ritual occasions—may likely represent a reaction to the trivialization of worship among the "avant-garde" organized churches. Employing coffee-cups and plastic plates, household dishes, supermarket food, wearing ordinary work or play clothes, playing the record-player, talking casually during the service, departing from prescribed ceremony—all running counter to the immemorial religious impulse of mankind—are felt by many to be sacrilegious, a profanation or "making common" of the sacred, which is essentially the extraordinary. Ageless custom requires that even a humble cup, once used for sacred service, must not be restored to domestic use without being de-consecrated or "secularized," and if that is not possible it must be destroyed.

Similar feelings undoubtedly simmer below the conscious hostility which many overtly religious people feel towards singing popular songs at Mass or worship services. For music is also consecrated by sacred function and to chant a hymn outside a holy service is anthropologically (*pace* Perry Como and Anita Bryant) as much a profanation as is bringing a popular ballad into church. (Oral Roberts and Billy Graham may be excused, because their television programs are sacred services for many Americans.)

The realization of the special character of sacred service is also behind the inclination to wear special clothing while performing or attending the rites Street dress visibly threatens to lower the ceremony to the pedestrian level. Language, too, when addressed to divinity or even to fellow worshippers in the context of adoration, should be special. Archaic idioms, apostrophic address, even the use of ancient language such as Greek, Latin, Slavonic, or Old Mandarin, as well as poetic style, sonorous cadences, and chant set speech itself apart from ordinary talk and establish an audible link with the past (a clue, perhaps, to the archaic level of much ecstatic speech incorrectly called glossolalia).

Needless to say, all of these tendencies are at most half-conscious attitudes in our liturgical experiences, for religion works for the most part on the unconscious level. It is just as well; self-conscious attempts at solemnity easily degenerate into cant: the pulpit tone and hypocritical rhetoric. But sensitivity is a two-way process—forgetfulness of the basic motives for custom can heighten the resistance to alter them, while the desire to revitalize liturgy can drive reforms across the threshold of banality into the profane. Religious power must be relativized by a healthy Christian iconoclasm, but the conscious split between conservatives and progressives is today a matter of a growing insensitivity to each others' needs and intentions.

At this point, it may be opportune to inquire to what point religion can be allowed to dominate Christian worship.

Religionless Christianity: Desacralization vs. Desecration

Since the publication of Dietrich Bonhoeffer's papers, contemporary theologians have argued cogently that religion can indeed become an oppressive institution, regulating and increasingly controlling the lives of Christians, and there should be retrenched. To the extent that organized religion deprives worshippers of the freedom of self-disposition towards the Holy and the opportunity to advance in the quest for transcendence, it is indeed a principality—a power of death. Dietrich Bonhoeffer, in the face of the Church's capitulation to Nazism, demanded a religionless Christianity freed from the bondage of the ever-increasing perfectionism of cult which hypnotized the devout into submission to all authority as divinely sanctioned. His disdain for the lifeless and therefore devitalizing worship of the organized churches of Germany has been echoed in the United States by William Stringfellow's Barthian invectives. Similarly, Heinrich Schlier has clearly demonstrated that the temptation of the Church to succumb to the domination of the principality of religion was a concern for St. Paul as much as it is for him.

Certainly, considering Christianity to be a religion has definite advantages—it assures the harmony of regulation and uniform observance, the comfort of historical continuity, freedom from fear of radical change, and so on. But there are tangible disadvantages as well. If, for instance, modern Christians' religious needs—which are quite distinct from faith—are more expertly satisfied by unofficial religions such as professional sports, the motion picture world, and professionalism, all of which have their sacred history, saints, traditions, rituals and rubricians, as well as plenty of pageantry—or through politics and science, which are religions to many—then it becomes a hopeless task for ministers and priests to compete for allegiance. The most successful religious leaders of the present era are, after all, politicians such as Ian Paisley, Bishop Makarios, Jesse Jackson, and the Berrigans, and who can deny that the achievements of Mahatma Gandhi and Martin Luther King were not primarily in the political order? (Even Billy Graham is a potent political figure among middle Americans.) Hence the justification for the rise of "political theology," the "theology of revolution," and so forth.

Could it be, then, that religion and Christianity are co-existent realities and often even antagonistic ones? Was the silence of the evangelists on matters of cult more than a question of emphasis

221

or editorial economy? What lay behind the slow evolution of the Christian priesthood?

Such questions demand much deeper investigation and more expert treatment than can be given here. Nonetheless, it is of significance with the purview of the occult revolution to consider that since religion is a fundamentally human response to the desire for personal self-transcendence and mystical communion with the wholly and Holy Other, it is therefore likely that religious practices will and perhaps must be present for an integrated human life, and framing the most important events—matters of ultimate concern such as birth and death, marriage and procreation, community solidarity, the trials of sickness and temptation and guilt. If Christianity represents an affair of moment for people, it will manifest religious characteristics because it, too, is human. But if religiosity and faith are nevertheless distinguishable, only an ongoing struggle keeps one from dominating the other. From the perspective of faith, it is always necessary to relativize the forms of religious life, subordinating them to the impulses of the Spirit. (The relative factors in Christianity, from a theological viewpoint, are cultural expressions, which always mediate the dynamics of faith and service; but they are always mutable, and in times of social and cultural transformation must change lest the inner meaning of Christianity be obscured.) But conversely, if the concern for purity of commitment threatens to suffocate the religious sensitivities of people, it is truly a Christian response to examine our style of life, for we have been manifestly desensitized to the real and pressing needs of our emphatically human brethren.

Liturgically, this means that resensitizing urban Christians, the building of community and the conscious will to celebrate, must be undertaken in earnest to protect the life of the Spirit within us. Liturgical vitality is the *result* of a truly Christian commitment, as relevance is more a sign than a cause of the real presence of the Church among men. This means, in turn, that unselfish attention to the needs of the world is the first prerequisite of valid worship, as relevance is the blush of health on the Christian countenance—both effects of being in tune with the whole of creation through affirming celebration.

Beyond Ritual: The Roots of Mysticism

By now it should be clear that a theme of this meditation is that the search for liturgical expression, interpersonal communion, and mystical union represent positively the driving force of the occult revolution. Emergent heterodox cults have emphasized these values openly, while the organized churches have manifestly despaired of each in one form or another. At least in the experience of the disaffiliated young, the churches have fallen in large part under the spell of the principalities of power, wealth, and prestige, becoming acolytes of Mammon rather than prophetical counter-culture agencies against whose life and teachings society can gauge its moral significance.

Despite the blossoming of guitar masses, banners, multimedia celebrations, dissident clergymen and sisters, activist rabbis and pastors, the youthful opposition is telling us that authentic worship, genuine authority, and true commitment have seemingly ceased to matter in the churches. What life is manifest seems to have spun off in the anomic disintegration of organized religion, leaving empty hulks. Hence the appeal of occult cults wherein it is possible to dance and sing, to seek mystical experiences and discuss them openly, to be turned on by Jesus or Satan or Selene or the stars rather than abstractions such as relevance, freedom, encounter, and confrontation (or, conversely, authority, tradition, and obedience)—all of which are mere words in view of the shallow lives of many churchgoers. The roots of integrated living and spontaneous joy are buried in the rich loam of our collective and traditional experience of the Holy and the beautiful and the true. Further, these qualities are themselves properties of the "other"—not primarily personal possessions of our selves.

All mystical teachers insist that one must lose himself before he may gain the higher realization of real and lasting love, communion and joy, that ecstasy is the condition of transcendence. And even though ecstasy cannot be coerced or purchased, but can only be received—even in induced states—it has always been accessible to those who were open to the adventure of the Quest. The paths towards transcendence are manifold but well-traveled in human experience throughout history. Through the perfection of the mind, by prayer, meditation, and contemplation, saints of every race and clime have achieved absorption in the Absolute Beyond—as witnessed in Christian mysticism, the Buddhist, Hindu, and Sufi "ways." Others have chosen the route of corporal ecstasy, gaining oblivious rapture in ritual dance, drugs, sex, chants, and the physical culture of yoga. Passive reception of enlightenment has gained unexpected beatitude for many—the enthusiastic experience of Saul of Tarsus, Mohammed, Gautama, the quest of the mystics of Port Royale, the Illuminati, the Quietists; call them what you will—Apollonian, Dionysiac, daimonic—ultimately the lived experience of the great mystics of humanity transcend the capacities of all experiential categories.

Mysticism also escapes the regulation of rubrical finesse and theological expertese and, consequently, the ecstatic experience has always been a touchy area among highly organized religions. And perhaps rightly so, because the possibility of delusion is great. Discernment of the presence of the Spirit is itself a gift of the Spirit and not to be had for the asking or purchase. But in times of distress, when the presence of the Spirit is most needed, the temptation to rely on the ever-ready expedients of technique, whether political control, intellectual authoritarianism, or mere custom, is also more compelling. Orthodoxy in belief and practice is demanded by those whose thrones are unsteady and in a proportionate degree: Quakers as well as witches were hanged in Protestant England and colonial America, and today, Catholic pentecostalism is viewed by many a jaundiced ecclesiastical eye.

Experience of the divine for most people, however, is not a matter of intensely ecstatic adventures, possible though that might be. Rather, the traditional furniture of religious observance is relied on to create a desired mood, the primordial womb of profoundest security. Familiar rituals and chants, whether intelligible or not, create a sacred filter which shuts out the cacophony of everyday life, allowing the uncluttered if unexpanded spirit to bathe in the refreshing rays of the supernatural. The peasant woman telling her beads or rapt in vacant beatitude at Benediction was perhaps a faint replica of the mystic Catherine of Siena lost in thunderous ecstasies of adoration. Yet because of the loss of meaning for most Catholics such traditional devotional forms suffered through routinization—particularly the rosary, Benediction, fasting, chant, processions, novenas, the veneration of relics, and the cult of the saints (which no doubt often plunged the unwary backwards into the magical world)—the crisis of the Church in the modern world doomed them to suppression. And properly so. Taking any of life's ceremonies for granted is an infallible method of losing their benefits and being left with hollow formalism, whether in religion, friendship, or social activity.

Future Flock

It is a bit shocking when anthropologists nevertheless tell us that liturgy, like everything else, has constantly changed through man's history. Cultural development, like natural evolution, at first occurred slowly, only a few elements being added or lost as whole generations passed. Over the long haul, such a similarity to organic evolution disappears; our traditions are fairly fluid in the longer perspective—only human life has always been a little more so. Since it changed so slowly, custom—the concrete memory of a people—seemed to be unchanging.

Within the past two centuries, moreover, the rate of socio-cultural change suddenly increased, passing the threshold of individual perceptibility. Under the aegis of the recent cybernetic revolution which is itself a function of technological progress and expanding population, the interval between major psycho-social changes began to shorten at an ever increasing rate. Simultaneously, people began living longer as medical progress continued, and communications improved our awareness of the world as a whole. Further advances, feeding off change in a geometric chain-reaction, created a feeling of what Robert Adolphs called "rapidation" and Toffler designated "future shock." We *feel* a growing inability to keep up-to-date; we find ourselves in wholly novel situations which have only vestigial resemblance to former conditions—the war in Indochina being a case in point. Today the future is hurtling at us with astonishing rapidity, a nemesis bulging with the consequences of present mistakes which we cannot cope with because we are still trying to unravel those of the past. The experience of being caught in the interface between what should be (but is not) and what will be (but should not) has dealt contemporary man a blow in the cultural solar plexus.

No wonder then that liturgy has been all but eradicated by our attempts to reorient the Church to the future-beset modern world. By nature a conservative (because religious) phenomenon, how can liturgy enable us to cope with the future? It seems sufficiently hard-pressed to deal with the present and really comfortable only with the past.

Several courses lay open before those intent on liturgical reform, but the time for decision among them is diminishing rapidly. By exaggerating the traditional elements of ritual and resisting all innovation, we certainly run the risk of dichotomizing life and worship ever further: ritualism, the extreme conservative solution, is therefore not the answer. We can attempt the polar opposite and constantly update our celebrations, adding every new theological catch-phrase and audio-visual novelty as it appears, adding readings from *Time* to the daily Gospel, and thus repudiate all connection with the past. But here we are relinquishing the entire heritage of humanity's history, including the very sources of Christian cult. We cannot inaugurate a new religion very easily—unless we can consciously recreate the past in so doing, and just leave out the past thousand years or so—the occult revolution. Actively or passively drifting from experiment to experiment in the hope of discovering a viable form of worship no less endangers our sense of continuity with the past and all hope of a future of foreseeable identification. Finally, we can give up and restrict our liturgical life to football games and hockey, or perhaps quit entirely.

Ritualism, rebellion, and withdrawal are inadequate responses for a liturgical reform true to the religious instincts of the race. The only other alternative is for us to do what every people has done to endure successfully the ravages of profound and sudden change: renew ourselves by simply and honestly trying to fulfill our destiny, to become what we are called to be by accepting life and affirming not only the future, but the present and the past as well. It is by no means easy to stay in tune with the world and have enough trust in ourselves and the Spirit within us to just "let it be," allowing our liturgies to develop from our shared experience of life and the wholehearted affirmation of its ultimate mysteriousness.

Liturgy is the official cult of a people, a community, and Christian liturgy is no different. To renew liturgy, we must renew the community, fashioning a people for God. In the midst of the desensitizing forces of the technological principalities, the pessimism of modern life and the monotony of urban existence, this rebuilding of community must be difinite and positive—a reawakening of the disorganized members of the churches to the dimensions of human and natural sensitivity, a reaffirmation of the totality of life, and its conscious and joyful celebration in both festival and fun.

Liturgical Sensitivity

If it is true that the answers to the liturgical impasse have to be found rather than programmed, that they result from living rather than precede it, then the following suggestions may make sense. They are merely suggestions, however, not panaceas. It will be necessary to work out from under the heap of rubrical rubble by dint of innovative experimentation, and the following represent possibly likely alternatives based on the foregoing meditation on the occult revolution.

First, since liturgy is the *ergos* of the *lais,* the work of the people, we must fashion a people with some collective identity and felt purpose. Ritual is not merely the performance of a scenario written by some expert, but the distillation in song and dance of "where we have come from, who we are, and where we are going." Amateurism is not preferable to skilled execution and a thorough understanding of what we are about, but it is the whole people who must be primarily engaged in their fullest capacity as a people, conscious of their origin and goal in history, their role in society, aware of the demands that their existence has placed before them at this moment and in this place, and willing to accept and affirm their responsibility for what befalls the world and its children—all of this prior to any "guidance" from experts.

Prophecy

History changes, no doubt of it, and what is expected of the people of God today is not what was demanded of them in the past, save that whatever the task may be, it will be achieved only by conscientious striving to remain faithful to the personal spirit of God in loving, radical obedience, which transcends every claim of law. Such fidelity would be impossible without the presence of prophets in our midst who see more clearly what is upon us and where the path of creative fidelity takes us. They are known by their word and works, measured against the whole history of God's self-revelation, the witness of Scripture, and the life of the Church. True prophecy, which is the juice and marrow of liturgy, is always consonant with the experience of God's presence, but its voice is not always a welcome sound in a world beset with human frailty, malice, and the perennial temptations to serve power, Mammon, and relevance. God's prophets speak with authority, however, fearing neither the judgment of men nor history.

But prophecy, as a charismatic event in the life of the Church, is an occasional experience and cannot be relied on to get us out of every mess. Nor can all prophetical activity be measured by its liturgical impact; the ethical dimension, for instance, is far greater. But liturgical vitality can aid us to remain sensitive to the voice of the prophet by stimulating our awareness of the significance of events, people, the manifold furniture of our lives and the world of nature.

Wonder

All religion, and consequently liturgy as well, begins in wonder and aims at reverential adoration and union with the divine in mystical ecstasy. No blade of grass can be of inconsequence to a truly religious man, and how much more marvelous does religion's focus enable the human personality to appear. The quest for "something beyond" must begin there, with what—and who—is at hand. Liturgy keeps sensitivity alive by hallowing the ordinary, embuing it with the power to evoke the One whose it is, not by profaning the sacred. To this end, moments of utmost livability are stressed in ceremony, those sacraments of every religion in which the humble elements of water, fire, salt, food, drink, and the human pledge become channels of sanctification.

Community

We return, then, to the life of the people, the need for community. In the wake of the discovery of small group experience, it is likely that liturgy will become a dual phenomenon in the Church of the future—an intimate, informal sharing of the small community and the public worship of the congregation, which must necessarily be more structured. Rather than an atomized conglomeration, this larger community should be an assembly—better, an incorporation of the smaller groups: classes in a school, parochial groups within a parish, parishes in a diocese, a convention of houses of sisters or priests, and so on. There is need and scope for both kinds of celebration.

In order to enable both styles of liturgical celebration to develop, a conscious effort at group sensitization will have to be made. The work of the minister or pastor must henceforward involve reawakening his parishoners to the world of nature and more especially to the dynamic encounter among groups of persons. Human-relations labs, T-groups, and encounter sessions are a partial solution to the dehumanization of liturgical celebration. Technological man has been alienated from the whole human world, however, not just interpersonal contact—but also in business, casual meetings, participation in mass affairs such as rallies and conventions. Besides sensitivity training, other activities such as political and social improvement campaigns, block parties, picnics, festivals, nature hikes, and community clean-ups, and many other projects and events are valuable ways of reawakening urban Christians to the personal and natural dimensions central to effective liturgical life. The ability to respond to the whole of life must be revitalized, and while liturgy itself is one "place" where this can occur, making worship into therapy profanes both.

Yea-Saying

Acceptance of life, its affirmation and celebration, are essential liturgical responses. In worship we ratify our historical existence and undertake the fulfillment of the promises of the past and the creation of hope for the future. We make no apology for the times, attempt no evasion of responsibility for what we as a people have made of life, or, rather, what we can still make of it, for liturgy must never detract from our ability to see what is lacking of accomplishment and change. Hope does not entail renouncing the present, but affirms its promise for the future and ventures to assure that this promise will be realized. Hope is an active involvement in life.

Play and Laughter

Celebration and festivity have become favored topics among religious writers of late and also among the professional entertainment industry (not surprisingly). Out of all the ink, claims, and counter-claims, a few themes have emerged which are of importance to an understanding of the liturgical implications of the occult revolution.

Josef Pieper, in his work *In Tune With the World,* has perceived that the prior condition of festivity and celebration is playfulness. Play, we are beginning to understand, is in turn a function of creative leisure, a hard saying for work-oriented urbanites, but demonstrably true (and amply evidenced) in the counter culture. Fantasy—the play of the imagination—and festivity (its "outering") are equally integral elements of true celebration.

Such thoughts are entertainingly and superbly developed in

Joseph McLelland's *The Clown and the Crocodile,* a whimsical but deeply theological and scriptural meditation of the religious—and therefore comic—view of life. McLelland fully appreciates the often appalling facts of life, symbolized by the monstrous Leviathan of Job, but he recalls that God made the super-crocodile to be his playmate. Therefore, he argues, the proper understanding of even absurd and horrible tragedies is that, for a Christian, the deepest failure is only a prelude to a triumphant *dénouement* (which may sometimes occur *after* the final curtain). Life, then, is a divine comedy, and—like the Fool of the Tarot—man is esentially a clown, a Chaplinesque victim of circumstances (like birth) he always manages to get the better of.

In contemporary literature, drama, and films, figures such as Zorba the Greek are wonderfully appealing to contemporary Christians. Especially as enfleshed by Anthony Quinn in the film of Kazantzakis's novel, Zorba is Man still able to lust for life after cataclysmic defeats, for he is rooted not only in the earth but in the fertile soil of human loves. And Zorba ultimately laughs in the face of tragedy and failure—more, he dances—because he knows that life is really a joke but one has to be a little mad to appreciate it. Not coincidentally, the Greeks of old called religious enthusiasm "the divine madness." Zorba the Greek is an archetype of religious man.

In his wonderfully ghastly little parable *Something Wicked This Way Comes,* novelist Ray Bradbury probes the occult world with a similar understanding of the human predicament. The sole weapon against which death has no barb and terror no power is laughter. We cannot laugh and fear at the same time.

Laughter is man's divinest comment on the preposterousness of life, as the hero of Heinlein's *Stranger in a Strange Land* discovers while contemplating the pathetically human antics of apes. But it has to be real laughter, not the empty crackling of the jaded nor the programmed mirth of television audiences. In *Lazarus Laughed,* Eugene O'Neill's occult passion play, not only does Lazarus respond to his new life with laughter, but his laughing is different, as changed as he is—deeper, more real, almost hypnotic, and definitely contagious.

Savoring life, then, and thus enabling affirmation and celebration to burst the tedious monotony of everyday routine is consequent on the perception of the deliciously incongruous experiences of merely being human. A truly religious Christian, freed from the power of the principalities of death, must have a sense of humor—he must refuse to take himself too seriously. And here perhaps is the greatest obstacle to the success of the occult revolution: it is too grim, too serious and forbidding. Black is not the color of life (at least in our cultural milieu). If their indictment against organized religion is to be heard, modern occultists will have to learn to appreciate what their opposition finds so hard to grasp: that they, too, are laughable, that even the pretensions of religion are farcical in the eyes of God.

Laughter is the signature of the divine in man, the proof of his spiritual nature and adequate comment on the corporeal raiment whose dissolution he is wont to dread. Laughter—the wholehearted, irrepressible, wonderful explosion of mirth—is the very music of creation.

Afterword

IF it is true that mankind's unconscious fears and the stresses of societal change are likely to be projected onto surrogates who can then be safely destroyed, it would seem logical in the midst of the greatest rate of social change civilization has ever experienced that a modern equivalent of witches and devil-worshippers would be evident—particularly in the more technologically advanced nations. Carl Jung, towards the end of his life, found precisely that to be true of the famous "flying saucer" scares that followed World War II and reached a peak of activity following the Korean War. UFO's (unidentified flying objects) have the merit of being recognizably technological, which is a clue to their psychological function as well as an effective screen against understanding.

Flying saucers and their "little green men" are the contemporary technological equivalents of witches and satanists who were feared so greatly in the sixteenth and seventeenth centuries and who had attributed to them all manner of superhuman powers—such as flying. (Woe betide the first visitor from outer space who does set foot on the earth!) And even if we regard the saucers as the craft of benevolent intelligences who hope to prevent our blowing up the world by the misuse of atomic power (recall the old classic film *The Day the Earth Stood Still* and Arthur C. Clarke's novel *Childhood's End*), the psychological mechanism of projection is the same.

But what are the UFO's that thousands of people have actually seen? What were the witches? How is it that Jonathan Swift knew of the twin satellites of Mars, and even rather accurately designated their dimensions and speed of rotation, when they were discovered only in 1878? What about contact with the dead? What about voodoo and apparitions?

To have treated all the elements of magic and occultism would take an encyclopedia. The preceding meditation was the result of some personal experiences over the past few years and was not intended to be a comprehensive account of even contemporary occultism (for which many better books are readily available) except as an indication of serious changes that have recently taken place in society and the Church. Consequently, many areas were only superficially surveyed, and others passed by entirely; particularly interesting avenues would have led to a study of poltergeist phenomena, a catalog of ESP experiences, flying saucers, and spiritualism. The whole realm of superstition is ripe for psychological and theological harvest. The role of monsters—werewolves, vampires, ghouls, and their cinematic kindred—would have been equal fun. But within our set limits, namely, the sociological and religious parameters of contemporary experience, the pursuit of these topics would have contributed little more to an understanding of the occult revolution.

The occult revolution is, of course, not really occult and not strictly a revolution, despite popular opinion and the claims of friends and enemies. It is a counter-ecclesial, anti-scientific response to the demands placed on today's youth to explore possible directions for future development, perhaps even survival. A return to a state of peaceful collaboration between science, magic, and religion, such as envisaged in *The Morning of the Magicians,* may be such an option for the future, and that *would* be a revolution. What is, I think, very clear from even this sketch of counter-cultural explorations is that we are evidently dealing with the beginnings of a new understanding of man's abilities and his place in the cosmos.

There are both positive and negative effects of delving into occultism—for every step into the future opens the possibility of new blessings and new banes. As a religious symbol, the occult is necessarily ambiguous and our response is correspondingly ambivalent—the dangers may well be worth the benefits. Jung maintained that man is forever beyond his own comprehension without taking into consideration his "shadow"—that other side of him that complements the phenomenal, conscious personality. So also with civilization, science, philosophy, and religion—their "shadows," which are always at least partially secret, serve to remind us that there is always more to know, more to do, and, above all, more to become. Magic and the occult, as well as religion, represent those shadows.

To build a future of hope, men of faith and wisdom must collaborate with those who possess knowledge and power; none of them can any longer afford the luxury of rejecting data, phenomena, and methods that do not satisfy their preconceived notions. The imperialism of scientific technology, undermined by the counter-cultural rebellion—including the "occult revolution"—must be disrupted for the sake of a new freedom of inquiry and experimentation. The occult itself can well shed some of the paranoiac veils which its practitioners have protected it with and still not lose whatever accumulated wisdom magicians and alchemists have salvaged from mankind's dim past. Men of faith as well as vision, such as James A. Pike, must also be willing to risk reputation and security to contribute to the creative revolution that will one day replace the anarchism of the two cultures.

Building a future to live in, then, will require great innovation and rebelliousness, a willingness—even a passion to cast off the dual yoke of superstition and subservience to the principalities of modern science. The problem before us is how to do so with an eye to conserving the heritage of the past and without falling prey to new dominations, without instituting new inquisitions and reigns of terror, without culminating in mere negativism,

236

whether Teilhard's Strike of the Mind or Marcuse's Great Refusal.

The solution lies, at least in part, in developing a pervasive sensitivity, or, as Norman O. Brown has called it, a "new sensibility"—heightening our awareness of the presence of "the other," constant receptivity, tuning oneself with the world—the only world, the real and total world. That kind of sheer openness or, if one prefers, radical obedience, can only occur in freedom from the bondage of ideologies, institutions, and images—the principalities and powers of this modern world of darkness. The consciousness of the young that something is radically wrong, particularly in the West, is liable to lead once more to an assault on society—a religious reformation and a political revolt reminiscent of the Protestant attempt to re-establish the kingdom of God on the ruins of Catholic Christendom. Charles Reich in *The Greening of America* has explored the salvific dimension of today's new movements among American youth, much as had Theodore Roszak in less theological categories. However lasting, real, and potent this crusade, and whether it is a true remedy for the apocalyptic malaise of Western civilization, remains to be seen.

Whatever the outcome, it is amply evident that the new sensibility has caught on among the young in the form of an amalgamated openness to romantic idealism, political activism, occult enthusiasm, and a cultic naturalism that must inevitably collide with the established interests of institutionalized society, the mother-culture. Perhaps the twentieth century's "children's crusade" will eventually be bought off by the moguls of fashion and the acolytes of capitalism, whose chief and apparently invincible weapon is the fad. Even so, the defeated, if not thoroughly corrupted by the wiles of Mammon, are not likely to forget the taste of new wine. In religious terms, they have had a glimpse of salvation.

Index

Abbadon, 129
Acts of the Apostles, 47f., 193
aether, 34
Age of Aquarius, The, 15
Albigensians, 104
alchemy, 51
American Society for Psychical Research, 174, 176
anomie, 179ff.
Antony of Egypt, St., 126
Apocalypse, The (see *Revelation*)
apocalyptic, 67f.
Apollonius of Tyana, 46f.
apotropaic magic, 31
Asmodeus, 129
astrology, 62ff., 77ff.
astromancy, 78, 149
Atlantis, 45, 165
augury, 148
Augustine, St., 52, 126, 195f.
Azazel, 131

Becker, Dr. Robert, 90
Beelzebub, 128
Behemoth, 127
Berger, Peter, 176, 198
Black Mass, 106, 120, 132
Blavatsky, Madame, 176
Bodin, Jean, 112
Bonhoeffer, Dietrich, 220f.
Boniface, St., 52
Bowen, Dr. E. G., 89
Brethren of the Cross, The, 131
Brown, Dr. Frank, 88
Burning Court, The, 183

Cabala, 36
Campanella, Thomas, 76
Campanus, Johann, 75
Canon Episcopi, 102, 104f. 108
Cathars, 104, 130f.
Cayce, Edgar, 21, 69f. 85ff., 149, 161ff.
cheirognomy, 150, 152

cheiromancy, 150
Children of God, The, 185f., 199, 201
Church of Satan, The, 137ff., 185
clairaudience, 175
clairvoyance, 172, 175
Clarke, Arthur C., 59, 237
contagious magic, 37
Compendium Malificarum, 106
cosmobiology, 85
Council of Ancrya, 102
Council of Constantinople (V), 177
counter culture, 183
coven, 110
Crowley, Aleister, 54, 135
cunning men, 55

Dashwood, Sir Francis, 135
Death, 208
demons, 40, 122f., 172, 195
dermatoglyphics, 153
Devil, The, 107f., 127
divination, 146f.
Dixon, Jeane, 21, 165ff.
Doyle, Sir Arthur Conan, 196
dreams, 148

Ebertin, Reinhold, 85
ecology, 9, 140
Enoch, Book of, 129
ephemeris, 80
esbat, 110
eschatology, 70, 74, 201f.
Estabrooks, Dr. G.H., 173
Eusebius, 101
exorcism, 124
extrasensory perception (ESP), 116, 158, 172, 198

familiars, 107, 119
fascinatio, 106
flying saucers, 236
Fox Sisters, The, 196
Fuld, Robert, 146

Gauquelin, Michel, 89
genius, 34, 83
ghosts, 39
glossolalia, 175, 185, 198, 225
Gilles de Laval, 132f.
gods, 39, 64
Greene, Graham, 132
grimoires, 54, 130
Gurney, Edmund, 174

Hamlet, 72
Hamlet's Mill, 63
Hair, 15ff., 25f., 58, 61, 72, 156, 203
halo effect, 158
Harvey, William, 36
Hermes Trimegistos, 42, 44, 52, 62
Hipparchus, 70
Holzer, Hans, 113f., 216f.
Hopkins, Matthew, 107
horoscope, 78ff.
houses, 77f.
Huntington, Dr. Ellsworth, 88
Huxley, Aldous, 9
Huysmans, J., 135
hypnotism, 173

I Ching, 147
idolatry, 195
imitative magic, 36
incubus, 123, 144
Innocent VIII, 111
Isaiah, 101, 127, 194
Isodore of Seville, St., 52

James, William, 174, 194
James I, King, 111f.
Jerome, St., 48
Jesus, 74, 177, 203, 209, 213f.
Jesus Freaks, 183, 198f.
Jesus Christ Superstar, 199ff.
Joachim of Flora, 103
Job, Book of, 123, 126, 234
John Chrysostom, St., 49
Jones, Marc Edmund, 6
Judaism, 67, 127, 194, 202, 204
Jung, Carl, 31, 72, 91, 124, 197, 207, 236

karma, 69, 86, 164, 177
Knights Templar, 105, 131
Krafft, Ernst, 89

Laing, R. D., 27
laughter, 235
LaVey, Anton, 121, 137f., 183

Lemuria, 165
Leviathan, 123, 127, 234
levitation, 175
Levi, Eliphas, 54
Lilith, 102, 123
liturgy, 218ff.
Lucifer, 127ff.
Luciferans, 108, 131

Magi, The, 20, 43f., 65, 155, 195
magic, 33, 40, 43, 188, 204f.
Maimonides, Moses, 130
Malinowski, Bronislaw, 32
Malleus Malificarum, 106
mana, 35f.
Manasseh, 100
Manson, Charles, 211
Maple, Eric, 119
Mathers, Macgregor, 54
May, Rollo, 205
McKuen, Rod, 25
Mead, Margaret, 27, 177
Merlin, 50
Merton, Robert K., 158f., 180f.
metamorphosis, 107
de Montespan, Madame, 133
Moody, Dwight, 163
moon, 89f.
Morning of the Magicians, The, 21, 188, 238
Murphy, Gardner, 174
Murray, Margaret, 110
Myers, Frederick, 174

necromancy, 126
Nelson, Dr. John, 88
Nephilim, 128
Nigeria, 118, 125
Nostradamus, 48, 54, 76

object reading, 172, 175
obsession, 35, 123
occult, 23f., 30, 204
oneiromancy, 148
oracles, 45
Order of the Golden Dawn, The, 56, 185
Order of the Silver Star, The, 56
Origen, 126
Origenism, 177
ouija board, 146

palmistry, 150, 151ff.
Paradise Lost, 143
Parrinder, Geoffrey, 118
Paul, St., 47, 208ff.

pentecostalism, 199
Peterson, Dr. Willam, 90
Phaeton, 63
Philip IV, 105
phrenology, 149
Piccardi, Dr. Giorgio, 88
Pike, Bishop James A., 21, 192f., 197, 215
planets, 66, 81f., 90f.
Plato, 44f., 210
play, 233f.
poltergeists, 123, 175
Porteous, A. C., 171
possession, 124, 205
Pratt, Dr. J. G., 174
Precession of the Equinoxes, 71f.
precognition, 175
priests, 40
Principalities and Powers, 206f.
Process Church of the Final Judgment, The, 121, 138ff., 183
progressions, 84
Prometheus, 63
prophecy, 169ff., 230f.
Ptolemy, Claudius, 75

Rahner, Karl, 170
reincarnation, 164, 177f.
religion, 41, 188
retrocognition, 175
Revelation, Book of, 36, 48, 102, 128f., 130
Rhine, Dr. J. B., 22, 173
Rosicrucians, 175, 185
Roszak, Theodore, 142f., 183
Rudhyar, Dane, 26, 85

Sabbath, witches', 107, 109
sacred, the, 219
de Sade, Marquis, 135
Satan, 126
Schlier, Heinrich, 207, 212, 221
Scot, Reginald, 111f.
sibyls, 45f.
sidereal zodiac, 73
Sidgwick, Prof. Henry, 174
signs, astrological, 81
Simon Magus, 47, 193
Society for Psychical Research, 174
solar year, 70
Solomon, 53
sorcery, 47f., 100
spirits, 38
spiritism, spiritualism, 196f.
stars, 90

Stetson, Dr. Harlan, 88
Stevenson, Dr. Ian, 174
Stringfellow, William, 207, 212, 221
succubus, 123, 144
sun, 88f.
supernatural, the, 38f.
superstition, 30
Swedenborgians, 196
Swift, Jonathan, 237
sympathetic magic, 36

Takata, Dr. Maki, 88
Tarot, the, 26, 83, 147, 155
tasseography, 150
Tchijewski, Dr. A. L., 90
Theodore of Canterbury, St., 52, 109
Theosophical Society, The, 176
Thomas Aquinas, St., 75, 149, 170, 195
Thurston, Herbert, 197
time, 74
Toffler, Alvin, 12, 189, 190, 228
transvection, 106, 119
tropical zodiac, 73
Turner, Mrs. Gladys Davis, 163
2001: A Space Odyssey, 59f., 63

Uranus, 93

Van Der Leeuw, G., 147
Vatican Council II, 10
Velikowski, Dr. Immanuel, 202
voodoo, 34, 136f.
votive Masses, 133

Waite, A. E., 56
"War of the Sorcerers," 36
warlock, 99
Watchers, The, 128
white magic, 97
William of Paris, 130
witches, witchcraft, 35, 96ff., 182, 184, 189, 216
wizard, 55, 99

xenoglossy, 175, 198

Yinger, Dr. J. M., 183
Yoga, 29, 175
youth, 203f., 214, 223, 238

Zen, 29
ziggurats, 65
zodiac, 66
Zoroaster, Zoroastrianism, 53, 123, 129